Trans/Love

- also edited by Morty Diamond -

From the Inside Out:
Radical Gender Transformation, FTM and Beyond

Trans/Love

**Radical Sex,
Love, and Relationships
Beyond the Gender Binary**

edited by
Morty Diamond

Manic D Press
San Francisco

To my wife,
my one sweet songstress and keeper of my heart,
you lift me higher, help me to dream, and make it all worth it

There is not a word, sentence or paragraph that can reveal my true appreciation to the writers in this anthology so I will simply say thank you on this page and hope to one day say it to each of you in person. Thank you to Jay and Leslie Diamond, Rhani Lee Remedes, Andres Bedoya, Jeanne Vaccaro, Bonnie and Chris Crum. To the transgender, transexual, intersex, two spirit, genderqueer, and gender variant communities, my love to you all.

Note: There are many varying ways to name differently gendered individuals. Certain terms may be preferable to some, but offensive to others. Please note that phrasing and usage has not been altered to fit the editor's preference. The distinct manner in which each writer names and describes their gender and preferred identity has been preserved.

Published by Manic D Press. For information, contact Manic D Press, PO Box 410804, San Francisco CA 94141   www.manicdpress.com
Printed in Canada

Cover painting:
"Embrace"(2009) by David Van Everen   www.davidvaneveren.com

Library of Congress Cataloging-in-Publication Data

Trans/love : radical sex, love, and relationships beyond the gender binary / edited by Morty Diamond.
    p. cm.
 ISBN 978-1-933149-56-1 (pbk. original) -- ISBN 978-1-933149-46-2 (ebook)
 1. Transsexualism. 2. Transgenderism. I. Diamond, Morty, 1975-
HQ77.9.T7153 2011
306.76'8--dc23
                    2011031464

Contents

Introduction

Transgender people maneuver in a world that seemingly offers little hope of finding love... or even good sex. If they aren't ignored and rendered invisible by mainstream narratives of romance, trans and gender-variant folks are consistently portrayed as deviants unsuitable to love. Prostitutes, impostors, freaks: these roles assigned to mainstream transgender characters help reinforce the normative gender binary that destroys any option for true gender fluidity in the world.

As familial, social, and personal changes abound during transition, a question arises early: *Who is going to date me now?* Or if currently partnered, *Will my relationship survive this transition?* Looking to popular media for answers will yield disparagingly dismal results.

This anthology was born from the determination to open a dialogue about transgender sex and sexuality, and the need to represent ourselves in this conversation. As a trans person, I wanted to put together our true stories of love and sex proving that we are not only loveable but charming, smart, and good in bed, too! *Trans/Love* is 29 transgender, transexual, two spirit, genderqueer, and intersex writers discussing sex, love, and romantic relationships, and how our gender identity shapes and interacts with these parts of our lives.

Although no anthology could give the full breadth of all the various identities and sexualities of trans love and sex, this book is a love letter to the trans community and beyond, hoping to add truth to the complex trans experience. I welcome you to read these pieces with as open a heart as the authors of the stories possess.

Moments of elation, heartbreak, and everything in between... trans people go through all of this within the flux of gender identity. As we navigate our way, all we can hope for is a little love, a little sex, and for those of us who dream of it, someone to call our one and only.

Enjoy,
Morty Diamond

Embodiment of Love
Morty Diamond

When I became a transman (female-to-male transexual), my frame of reference regarding mutual attraction and having a love life changed drastically. Formerly dyke-identified, as I worked to understand and reformulate my new gender identity I figured I could throw everything I learned about finding sex and love as a woman out the window. Even though I lived in San Francisco, a place seemingly overrun with trans people, I wasn't quite sure who was going to date me. Ultimately, my life would be filled with romance found on city streets, in bars, and through the Internet, with much less struggle than anticipated.

To help paint the picture of how I explored my gender identity within my relationships and sex life, I would like to point out the two women that have made the biggest impact on my life, Kate and Rachel. Without the kindness, openness and trust of these two women I would have struggled much longer to find equilibrium in my body and mind. These two loves were especially poignant during the physical and emotional transition into my own version of manhood. Kate was there in the beginning, as my transition gained traction, meeting me a week after I changed my name to Morty. Rachel was there at the end, when I reached my final destination with acceptance and love for the trans person that I had become.

I met Kate on the streets of San Francisco in the late '90s, a time of dotcom money and a new burgeoning trans community. Be it luck, fate, or whatever brings two people together, this was a match made to last. A pair of Scorpios, eyes shining bright with lust for each other, we rollicked in the streets filling our hearts with all that our young love was about: dancing, drinking, blood, scars, and killer sex. Even though my male identity was only tentatively bubbling forth, it seemed to be the last thing on our minds when we were together. I cannot recall one moment when I had to explain myself or qualify my feelings about who I was becoming.

I was simply Morty, her tranny man, and she was my girl, herself a bit skewed from traditional gender norms.

A high femme warrior, always dressed to the nines in high heels and blood red lipstick, Kate exuded strength and humor. When men would mess with her on the street, she would tell the guy to fuck off while laughing right in his face. She taught me the art of holding my own, be it in the streets or at some tedious temp job, she told me to never compromise myself for anyone. And I didn't.

Soothing me with reassuring words, Kate was the woman who held me as I injected my first shot of testosterone. The first six months of being on T were tumultuous. Within the first three months, I was thrust into a second puberty, complete with acne, and a voice that cracked every other sentence. I also experienced head and muscle aches as my body adjusted to the new surge of male hormones in my bloodstream, and during the times I felt like a wreck, Kate put me back together. She soothed my senses when they were frayed and became my cheerleader simply by staying in love with me while I melded myself into the person emerging. I am convinced that Kate ferried me to the other side when I could not do it alone.

Our love was complicate and within the five years we were together many facets of our personalities were revealed, both gorgeous and terrible. The one thing that stayed true was our ability to see beyond gender. Knowing ourselves, it came as no surprise that we had an emotionally intense breakup. I regret very few things in my life but the way the relationship ended tops that short list. Kate will always be the woman that, in my fledgling moments of becoming trans, supported me and allowed my transition to be filled with a glowing, exuberant love.

After Kate, I believed I would never again have such deep love in my life. I just didn't think it was possible for a guy like me, whose trans experience did not follow the normal trajectory. Most trans people I know go on hormones and have surgery as soon as possible. I had waited over a year to begin testosterone and another three years until I decided to complete my transition with a double mastectomy (or chest surgery). Since beginning to identify as transgender I have struggled almost constantly with my gender identity. I will never forget meeting a psychic before I even thought of transitioning who said to me, "You know you don't have to choose between being male and female." In that moment I didn't understand what she meant, but years later, I do.

After being on testosterone, or T, for more than five years, I concluded that the hormones were not working for my mind, body, or spirit. Initially, I took testosterone because I wanted to stop living as a woman. Use of this hormone afforded me the ability to transform my appearance and legal gender but after awhile I realized that my maleness did not come from a weekly injection. Discontinuing testosterone but still living and being publicly accepted as male, I struggled to reposition myself as a trans person who sported a thick beard while getting his period. During this second transition, I also worked to redefine my sexuality in terms of my newly adjusted gender identity.

Shortly after my decision to stop using testosterone, I moved from New York City to Los Angeles, an area with which I was completely unfamiliar. I found myself searching for the queer community so I put up a personal ad on Craigslist looking friends and perhaps a date. Rachel answered this ad and we emailed introductions that quickly became flirtations. Many keystrokes later, I asked her out on a date. Actually, I asked her out on what I called a "non-date" because, honestly, has anyone ever had a good date from a Craigslist ad?

The moment I set eyes on her I knew it. "It," as in, I knew that she was the one. I spent the next few hours of the date fighting this all too real but very frightening feeling. Truth was, I never had faith in the possibility of knowing love this immediately, or even of the idea of having a one true love. I didn't trust in the prophecy of my own heart. Yet there I was awake at 3 a.m. the morning after our first date writing in my journal, "I want to marry this woman."

Rachel managed in the course of a few months to look deep into my soul and search out all the nooks and crannies I kept hidden. I couldn't help it; I was laid as bare as a newborn on a bearskin rug as soon as she started to kiss me. We would read each other's minds and start to play these parts in bed that were, before meeting her, completely off limits for me. All of a sudden this clarity emerged in the unleashed spaces that sex with Rachel took me: I wanted to explore sex that allowed my female energy and sexuality to bloom but because I was so afraid of what that meant to my masculinity, I had for some time shamed and ignored this desire.

The first time I allowed myself to explore sex with Rachel while inhabiting both my masculine and feminine spirit was a deeply opening experience. For far too long I made decisions on what I was going to do in bed based on fears of being seen as too feminine or like my past female self in any way. Rachel gave me the space to let go of all the sexual baggage I carried, her hands pressing into me, coaxing and unraveling all the hard wiring I had in place. A blooming and also crushing rush of feelings raged through me and my jaw clenched from the yearning and fear. Yet, as natural as anything could be, this woman was peeling me open, layer by layer, taking me there. I fought to be open and forgiving, to allow myself to go where my desires were taking me. I needed to accept that just as my masculinity did not depend on the hormones in my body, it also did not hinge on the way that I had sex. For the first time, I got lost in the moments of being touched without gendering what was taking place. Rachel's refusal to accept only one facet of my sexuality helped me to reemerge as a fully formed sexual being, one who can inhabit female, male, and genderless spaces while having the best sex of my life.

Rachel is an absolute wonder in all of the everyday moments that make life worth living. Her presence in my life proved something I had previously regarded as impossible: that two people can find each other, even online, and make a connection that is otherworldly. Our love grew so deep so fast I sometimes think we shared a love so great in the past that it desired more time to be together in the future. I give myself a little pat on the back for allowing myself to listen to the inner workings of my heart, leave New York City and meet her on the streets of West Covina on a hot day in May.

Tattoo
Sam Silverman

I couldn't believe it. It was really happening. I opened my eyes and
Maia was still there, still on the bed in her little brown room with the
little pink trim, pursing her puffy movie star lips as if in slow motion,
moving in closer and closer for a second kiss. *I'm officially making out with
the hottest girl in San Francisco.* I reached around her back unbuttoning
the cute fitted shirt with two little birds carrying twine stitched on the
front pocket, and lifted it over her head. *She has such good style.* I leaned
in and kissed her again, and a rush of pride and accomplishment washed
over me. I undid her bra in a quick single-handed maneuver that I hoped
was impressive. *Don't tell her she's beautiful, stupid. Not yet.*

I looked at her naked torso the way a tourist stranded on a foreign
street corner scans a map: quickly, desperately, slightly embarrassed to
be so clearly lost. I traced the colors and patterns inked on her chest with
my finger, trying not to seem intimidated by the elaborate and detailed
landscape of her tattoos. I felt like I needed a key to understand what
they all meant. She pulled me back into her and I lay on top of her,
kissing her neck and face gently. I felt shy and nervous, not the slightest
bit aggressive.

We kissed a while like that until I started to feel like we were
characters in a Jeanette Winterson novel. I wondered if she wanted me
to start biting her or get rough. I figured it was time to interrupt our
lesbionic make-out session and take the plunge. I took off my shirt.

"You're a man!" She scooted away, eyes fixated on my chest.

My transition had been so gradual that it always shocked people to
see the scars around the tiny nipples that had already been on ice twice
in my life. First during a breast reduction that I hoped would be enough;
again after almost two years of binding my new perky B-cups that my
doctor insisted were proportional to my "wide and unfeminine" body
frame.

In a gesture that seemed part curious, part horrified, Maia traced the outline of the two thick scars that almost met in the middle of my body. There was still some evidence of the stitching underneath, little white lines that puffed up slightly in a webbed pattern echoing the stretch marks that they replaced. She looked mournful, and for a minute I thought she was going to cry.

"I'm not a man," I tried to reassure her, omitting the word "yet."

Maia was a true femme, a stone femme perhaps. I wasn't sure what that meant but I knew every straight guy with a pulse wanted to fuck her. A relief after my last girlfriend, who in many ways had been so much butcher than I was, always fixing things in those ugly Carhartt overalls, a wrench in one hand and a cigarette in the other. Maia was part of a group of femme dykes who even I could hardly believe were queer. When I thought about her friends sleeping with each other, the question that had once felt like a crude solipsistic male viewpoint now made a fair amount of sense: what *do* they do in bed together? Granted, these ladies seemed to prefer dating a very specific type of butch, but they also seemed to have taken an oath not to date men, identified or otherwise.

"Why? Do you like playing with little girly titties?" I teased. It felt good to be joking around. I relaxed a little, not feeling quite as desperate to impress.

I air-grabbed what had long ago been two pendulous D-cups and fake fondled them with my hands like a stripper. I thought about how if I still had my tits, chances were I wouldn't be in Maia's bed right now. If she could have seen me with those bovine danglers, with my near-soprano voice and everything slightly more rounded, I knew she never would have taken a second glance. The testosterone I had been taking in very small amounts for the past six months had just barely qualified me as butch enough for a date with Maia, and it had given me the balls to ask her out.

"Noooo!" She shook her head and rolled over. "But I wouldn't have minded them. I might have even tried to cop a feel every now and then, like I used to with Moe."

Moe, Maia's ex-wife, the butch police officer whom I often saw flexing huge biceps and old school tattoos in the mirror at the gym, her stringy long hair always pulled back in a ponytail. Moe was probably 15 years older than me, and I guessed she might have transitioned if she'd been closer to my age. In any case, I could not imagine Maia playing with Moe's breasts. It was not a pleasant thought. Ponytail or not, Moe was a guy to me, and I respected her maleness too much to think about her nipples. I tried to change the subject.

"So, when did you get that one?" I pointed to a tattoo that stood out from all the others. The initial intimidation had worn off, and I decided that her arms and chest were much more legible than I had previously thought. She was all hearts, swallows, banners, and X marks the spot. It was like any Mission back alley graffiti in San Francisco, a treasure trove of old timey, vaguely nautical, and bird heavy imagery. Still, I had to admit I liked them. I hadn't dated many girls like Maia and she made me wish I had more tattoos than the single child's drawing of a dead cat that I had found so minimalistically endearing in my 20s. Of course, the tattoo of hers that I liked best was barely noticeable, a tiny arrow on her lower back pointing down. She smiled, and I pulled her underwear down just slightly so I could see what it pointed at. Tiny lower-case letters spaced apart spelled out a word over one of her butt cheeks. *L-e-z-z-i-e*. A tiny heart dotted the letter i.

I sometimes feel like I'm right on the cusp of a generation where everyone's transitioning. Most of the East Coast butches I know have already become men who you'd never recognize as trans, but a lot of my SF friends still enjoy doing things like silkscreening t-shirts that read "Heart Yr Tits" and giggling about strap-on sex. The Moe brand of old-school butch was something I had witnessed but not exactly been a part of. I remember first seeing a bunch of butch dykes in San Francisco in the early '90s and wondering how they got that way. Mostly I wanted to know how many packs a day they smoked to get that low-voiced, husky quality of being butch that no amount of chain smoking and whiskey drinking was ever seemingly going to grant me. I felt hopelessly trapped in the body of a fifteen-year-old boy who hadn't quite hit puberty and never would. But I was determined to smoke and drink my way into some version of passable manhood. I was already almost thirty by the time I realized there were other, more effective means to achieve that end.

With Maia, my general sense of masculine inadequacy was further complicated. Here I was not only feeling like I had just barely made the butch lesbo cut, but I distinctly felt, despite her pronounced homosexual identity, that I was somehow not man enough for her. Everything about her screamed "fuck me with your big fat cock" and yet these six little letters seemed to spell our doom. I knew somewhere inside the minute I saw them that we wouldn't last long, and it hurt. Our first date and I already liked her so much.

"Cute." It was all I could muster. It came out pretty disingenuous but I didn't care. This was really the icing on the cake. Not only was she the hottest, straightest-looking girl I had ever been with but she was the gayest, too. I couldn't help wanting to blurt out something like, "Is that to make sure you don't forget?" Instead, I started rubbing her feet, hopeful that we could get back to the making-out part and stop reflecting on our glaring differences.

I rubbed her feet with a lot of intensity, as though I was communicating directly with her inner core self. I had a lot to say to her and this was my chance. I wanted her to feel my strength, to sense my attention to detail, to notice the way I spent time on and between every toe, every crevice. I moved my hands in small circles all over, pulling the skin around the balls of her feet taut. *I am opening her heart chakra.* I moved my hands up inside the crease of her foot, pressing firmly in upward strokes. *I am opening her mind.* She closed her eyes and looked like she was really getting into it. *Just imagine what I can do to the rest of you...*

And then it happened. Before I even had enough time to register what was really taking place, Maia had flipped me over and was starting to touch me. I seemed to have inspired some kind of competitive response. Suddenly she was on top of me, pinning me down. It felt weird. She felt heavy on top of me and I felt somehow dwarfed by her. She seemed so big all of a sudden. And her hands were going everywhere. First, they were on my chest and then on my belly and then creeping down to my thighs and it was all happening so fast. I tried to touch her back but I couldn't keep up. Every time she touched me I *had* to touch her back with even more intensity. It was a contest. It was impossible. She sensed my discomfort and stopped, looking up at me.

"Are you, like, getting all *Stone Butch Blues* over there?"

It was a cheap shot at my already fragile manhood, quickly dispersing in the wind of her lesbian glibness. I could have said yes but I was so smitten already that I couldn't bring myself to reject her. I didn't want us to stop having sex just because I was having issues, even though this was far from what I was used to and way outside of my comfort zone. I wasn't about to risk ending our make-out session by bringing up my butch boundaries.

"Um, no. I just don't do this... very often."

There. She could feel special now. I shot back with the only ammunition I could muster: sincerity. Now I had chosen her above all others to have a moment of free reign over my body. It was my idea to let her do this. Then I could turn the tide in a minute and all would be as it should, me on top and her writhing underneath. *Let her have her little moment of feeling in control.*

"Good," she said.

And so she began again, now even more aggressive than before. Her hands were all over my back and ass and then they moved back up to my chest and her face started a descent past my belly. With only seconds of foreplay on the clock she was already moving in for the kill! I would never dare to move so quickly were I on top. Had the woman never heard of foreplay? I had a brief thought of how perfect it would be if she could now be greeted by my huge erection. I wanted it to poke out through my pants sideways and smack her in the face, thick and swollen and already dripping a little pre-cum.

The reality was a bit different. My one-inch boner had long since deflated. I was glad at least I had decided to pack that day, although the Mr. Softie I had chosen was starting to look a little worse for wear. It had melted a little at the tip from too much time in its powdered plastic baggie, and had faded from pink into a dingy brown. I tried to remember the last time I had trimmed my pubic hair. I wondered if I smelled bad.

It occurred to me that maybe she was checking to see if I'd had bottom surgery. After the surprise up top maybe she just wanted to be sure. She didn't need any more surprises, I granted her that. She'd have herself a little sniff around and then she'd pop right back up for air and a proper fucking.

Maia went from sniffing around to poking around fast, and I was just about at the end of my femme-on-top tolerance rope when she had tossed Mr. Softie on the floor and crammed a few fingers up inside me. No buildup whatsoever. Maybe this was how she justified fucking a trans guy on the first date. No swirly-girly action, no soft caresses for me, no sir. If I was going to be a man, I was going to take it like a man. So take it I did, eager to prove that I could handle whatever she dished me, as long as the tide would eventually turn.

About six seconds into her eager poking session, a curious feeling overcame me. I felt my insides flip around and do a double-take. My face got very hot. I felt a steep descent like a drop on a rollercoaster, and then a numbness, and then more feeling than before. I inhabited myself both less and more in alternate turns. Something had shifted. I forgot about foreplay.

I didn't want to like it. I kept trying to leave my body to orbit the room from above, to watch myself get pummeled by that girl from a safe distance, but I was right there inside my body the whole time, feeling everything. She began to gather momentum, enjoying her power over me. I knew what was coming. Pretty soon she had shoved way past what I thought was possible and was up inside me as far as she could go. I closed my eyes and tried to become her, looking back at myself like a stuck pig. *So this is what it feels like. Slow can be better than fast,* I noted, feeling drugged.

When she was done, after my Vulnerable Moment and the clenching and eventual release, I lay there feeling like a deer run over by a car that kept on driving. I was sure something was oozing out of me so I tilted my hips up to keep it off the bed. My eyes were leaking, my cunt was leaking, and it felt like everything generally had a sad point to it. The picture on the wall of the girl in the rocking chair that had seemed old timey and quaint an hour before now seemed like the most depressing image ever.

I reached down to pull up my tighty-whities, relieved to cover myself. Maia looked at me like a stranger in her bed. I felt like a stranger, too, but we kissed anyway, glossing over the awkward intimacy that lingered in the air. Among other things, I wasn't used to coming first and realized for the first time that sex was hard to keep doing after you'd already come. But my turn on the bottom had illuminated some of the finer points of fisting, and I used these fresh techniques to my advantage. I gathered my strength and made sure that she came at least three times more than I had.

Months later when I would temporarily go off testosterone because I thought I was in love with Maia and wanted nothing more than for her to dot her heart with my i, I would think back on this night somewhat differently than it had been experienced, as The Last Great Resistance. I would herald this first fisting as a proper introduction between me and my uterus, with whom I had been formerly, unfortunately, unacquainted. I would deem archaic the 21st century transman who didn't love getting fucked by a femme once in a while, and proclaim like a penetration poster-boy: Try it, you'll like it! I would even renounce my trans identity for a time, convinced that my renewed faith in the functions of my extraneous body cavities equaled a return to womanhood. I would even welcome the blood back, holding it up in the women's restroom in its little cup that kept it from turning brown, and like a porn star awestruck at the sight of his own semen, marvel at the sheer amount of it that I was capable of producing.

And then, after all of that, we would break up anyway.

Confessions of a Bisexual Shemale
Vera Sepulveda

I get around. Call it what you want: promiscuity, nymphomania, loose morals, whatever. The bottom line is that I enjoy sex. It's taken me a while to get to this point, to be able to make that statement in print, for God's sake, and mean it. I like the flirting, the closeness, the different kinds of people I see, touch, and sleep with. I like men, I like women, I like the various flavors of in-between. We're all just people and we all have the same wants and desires no matter how we realize them. I like sharing my favorite human function with a fellow human being: scratching our mutual itch against each other.

I accept the label of "Bisexual" out of convenience, but in truth I'm more complicated than that. There was a time I only slept with women... when I was a man. After beginning my transition, I went through a phase of sleeping only with other trans people. Later I discovered the pleasure of sleeping with men and entered into yet another phase. In my life, phases have always been my method of gaining new experiences. I try new things, I experiment; I try other things. My life is anything but boring.

The latest phase, my Bisexual Phase, is different in that it's more inclusive. Rather than moving on to something new, I'm embracing all my previous experiences. Why not? None of my former experiences were unpleasant; rather they were reflections of certain points along my journey. Now that I've more or less settled at the current point in my transition, it seems only natural that I should look back to the experiences that helped form my sexual self, right? Well, it sounds good, but I never actually sat down and thought it all out like that before. I am not one to rationalize or justify my actions. How I entered this phase was much simpler than that. Something happened.

I have been cruising online personal ads for some time now, and I've met a lot of different people and partners in the process. I met my first man online. Frank and I dated for a while, fucked for a while, and had some great times together. We agreed up front that it was just for kicks. He had a steady girlfriend at the time and they enjoyed an open relationship that was fine with me. My quest to find lovers was never a quest to find love. Frank and I had fun for a while and everything was great, or so I thought, when things started to get complicated.

Frank's girlfriend, Jane, is interested in transexuals. When Frank tells me this, I'm intrigued. He senses the wheels turning in my head and says he'll talk to her about a possible threesome. Talk becomes plans and we soon go out to dinner together. It's my first threesome date. Jane and Frank seem very much alike and I sense they are a well-matched couple. We enjoy a pleasant meal and then go back to their place.

Previously Frank and I were in the practice of smoking pot while watching cartoons until I could no longer keep my hands to myself. But this time nobody seems inclined to smoke and hands were all kept to their owners. As the odd wheel in the threesome, I don't feel it's my place to initiate any friskiness nor do I feel any invitation to do so. Eventually someone announces that they're tired and going to bed. I take the hint and say my goodnights.

Needless to say, I'm disappointed. I had really warmed up to the idea of sleeping with the two of them. In addition to lots of sex, we could have had a nice sleepover and maybe a big breakfast. The social possibilities seemed so attractive. I email Frank a couple of times and when he finally replies, he ends it. He has been feeling awkward about things and thinks it best we call it quits. I assure him there are no hard feelings and thank him for some very nice times. I go back to cruising the personals with a new goal in mind: to find a couple.

Cruising the personal ads can be daunting. I prefer browsing other people's ads to posting my own ads, which tend to be pretty specific and generate very few responses. Craigslist has a neat system for categorizing sexual types according to orientation. Using terms like M4F, M4M, and M4MW, you can run a search of all the personal ads for specific types of connections. While many online dating sites use this sort of classification, Craigslist goes a step further by adding the T category for Transpeople. I search T4T when I'm in the mood for another tranny; MW4T when I'm looking for a couple that is into trannies. These usually bear scant results since I'm searching among a very small minority within a minority but once in a while I get lucky... in the full sense of the word. Oddly enough, I never search M4T. I used to, and the postings average between 20 and 30 a day. Plenty to choose from by any standard, yet reading the ads you discover that they are virtually all the same thing: guys who have a fetish for trannies. Now, don't get me wrong; I love guys who are into trannies but being objectified as a fetish isn't what I want. I see a huge difference between guys who are into trannies and guys who want to fuck a sex object. I don't want to be thought of as just a chick with a dick. I want to be a great girl with a great sense of humor, a good cook, and a relevant artist who's uncommonly exotic between the sheets. I want a friendly and social interaction even if it's based entirely on sex.

After a week or so of searching, I find an ad that seems right up my alley. An established couple consisting of a genetic woman and a part-time MTF tranny is looking for another tranny to form a threesome. I answer with a short email telling them about myself and include a picture. I get a response that includes their pictures, and we all agree that we like what we see so far. We set up a meeting in a public place: a coffee house in my neighborhood. This, along with stipulations about safe sex, is standard procedure for online connections.

We hit it off immediately. They are older, which is a refreshing change from my usual attraction to people much younger than me. For once, I am to be the young plaything. I find that role reversal intoxicating. We chat a bit over coffee then walk back to my place. Lucy, the woman, is full figured and voluptuous. Chris, the tranny, is tall and slim. My body seems like an averaging of their two extremes. Friendly chat gives way to touching and kissing. Soon we are in bed together.

When I tell people that I like threesomes, the questions they ask are usually mechanical. People accustomed to one-on-one sex often think that someone has to be left out, merely waiting their turn to have a go. While I'm sure that could be the case with some, it has never been the case with me and my friends. The bed is full of breasts, genitals of all sorts, six hands, and three mouths. We move among each other, slipping in and out of the coveted middle. Abstractions like "top" and "bottom" lose all meaning when the two-player dynamic is removed. We form a sort of a sexual communism in which all participants offer their unique gifts according to their individual attributes, to be shared and enjoyed by all.

Time passes quickly. After hours of playing, the pace slows to cuddling and kissing. Clothes are retrieved from around the room, talk turns to more worldly matters, and we all agree to meet again. And we will. Lucy and Chris leave me glowing and ecstatic. The culmination of my fantasy has turned out better than I would have ever hoped for. After years of drought in my previous male life, I realize that my sexual identity is beginning to form itself anew, according to my new anatomy and personality. I love it.

My body seems built especially for sex. Maybe "engineered" is a better term since I have undergone hormone therapy these past several years. I am tall and slim; maybe "athletic" would be more descriptive but I'm not athletic. I have picked up several pounds since beginning hormones, and although my doctor warned me to watch my weight, I can't help loving how good those extra pounds have been. My breasts are not huge but prominent. My nipples are pink and puffy. Spironolactone has purged most of the hair from my body. My skin is soft and smooth; I avoid the sun and use SPF 50 sunblock at the beach. Fat has redistributed to smooth out my angles, pad my hips and ass, and although I have a bit of a paunch, it is distinctly feminine. My penis has shrunk somewhat, another effect of the hormones, but still works wonderfully. I feel that its cuteness suits my personality better than my old one. I have had no complaints. To sum it all up, I'm a kid who got the whole candy store. Everything I wanted is mine, in better quantity and quality than I would have dared hope. I am a shemale: the perfect fusion of male and female. In financial terms, I am a sexual millionaire.

Unfortunately, there are logistical problems with my new relationship. Part of the difficulty inherent in threesomes is communication. Lucy and Chris do not live together. I correspond with Lucy, but she needs to confer with Chris before getting back to me, which creates a delay. A couple of rounds of email can easily span a week. Then there is scheduling to consider. I have weekends free; Chris has only Sundays. Lucy is working on her master's degree, and is often busy. Still, the frustration is well worth the rewards.

The relationship is complex. They are an established couple, having been together some time before meeting me. They are in love. I am not expected to fall in love with either of them. I am not an equal partner in the sense of being one among three equals. In fact, there is no equality in this arrangement unless it is between the two of them. I am a mutual plaything—a fuck toy. If you describe our relationship as a triangle, it is not equilateral. Our triangle is isosceles. I am at the far apex while they form the base. This may sound unfair, perhaps even abusive, but it's not. If all sex were based on equality, it would be boring. Our sex is anything but boring.

I like the freedom of this arrangement. There are no entanglements. I'm not looking to score with one behind the other's back nor am I interested in inserting myself into their Relationship (capital R). I have my own emotional attachments that I keep separate from sexual adventures. I just love playing with them and that's all we want from each other.

We see each other off and on for a few months. They take me out dancing. I enjoy being with both of them together. There is an exhibitionistic aspect for me and possibly for them. I will sometimes step between them and put my arms around them both, kissing them each on the cheek. People notice. I suspect they enjoy it. A guy asks me to leave with him but I tell him I'm here with my date, "That cute couple over there." I am in heaven.

But eventually a rift opens. I get a call from Lucy. She is upset at something Chris said and thinks he's drifting away from her. I try to be reassuring but I'm out of my territory. I don't trespass on their emotional ground and I don't want to start. All I can offer is reassurance, which is totally unfounded in spite of its sincerity. And just like that, my relationship is in trouble. The irony is that it's not my fault. Through no action of my own, my couple is in danger of breaking up. Since I have no part of their Relationship, all I can do is hope my beautiful balloon doesn't break.

Of course, it does. I ran into them some time later. Happy hugs were exchanged. We never officially called it quits but we all knew when it was over. They worked out their problems, or at least are working on them, and are still together. I sometimes wonder if I was the problem they had to work out. It takes a strong relationship to withstand the stormy seas of a ménage à trois. I have never yet encountered a relationship that can.

There is a bisexual aspect of sex with another transexual that I find arousing. I have had a few relationships of this type. While none lasted, they were all spectacular. Although all were much younger than me, I don't think age was the issue. There is a competitive dynamic that exists among transexuals. We tend to judge ourselves based on how we compare to others of our species. Feelings of inferiority and superiority are poison to a relationship. Some trannies have issues about being touched in certain ways, which was the case in two of the instances. Rather than relationships, I prefer to think of these encounters as "affairs" or "flings." Nice for what they are, but I want more than just cotton candy.

Before too long, I find another ad that looks promising. A couple is coming to town for the Folsom Street Fair, San Francisco's best known public sex event, and wants to find a tranny to accompany them. Burt and Margie are about my age, incredibly sexy, and really nice people. Margie is six months pregnant. I suspect that I am to be something of a surrogate for Burt. We meet at their hotel and hit it off immediately. Margie is as big as the Graf Zeppelin, with huge breasts and swollen nipples. She is the first pregnant woman I've ever been in bed with and I am totally turned on by her exaggerated sexuality. Burt is, too, and for a while Margie is the focus of our attention. As the night progresses, Margie tires and the focus shifts to me. As I suspected, Margie is just too big to make penetration practical. Burt very nicely and very effectively nails me to the mattress. It's the best dicking I've ever had and I let him know it. I'm not exactly a screamer but I do make a big fuss. People in the next room may have been disturbed.

As we are recovering, Burt invites me to come spend a weekend. He offers to buy the train ticket and pick me up at the station. I am delighted. I offer to cook a big dinner and breakfast in bed. He is enthusiastic. Margie is in the bathroom at the time so I don't know what she thinks about all this.

In the early hours, I go back to my apartment in a sleepy daze. A few hours later it's time to meet up with Burt and Margie for the Fair. I call but get voicemail. I call again later—same thing. Finally I leave a message that I'm going ahead and hope to see them there. But among 400,000 people I have little hope of finding them. I have a great time partying with my fellow freaks, but I'm a little sad I didn't find my new couple. I email them later, telling them how much fun I had and how I look forward to seeing them again.

A few days later, I get an answer. Margie wasn't feeling well so they lay low and met up with some friends. They thank me for a wonderful time but no mention is made of my coming to visit. So it goes. I suspect that Margie was uncomfortable with Burt's enthusiasm and I can't blame her. I didn't want to intrude but how could I have helped it? Were I in Margie's place, I would probably feel the same. Once again it was a lovely experience, even if only for one night.

The nuances of sexual attraction and the subtleties of emotional involvement are fascinating. I'm attracted to men more often than women but my attraction multiplies exponentially to the idea of both at the same time. With a woman, my role can be confusing. Does she think of me as a man? Does she expect me to perform like one? If she's a lesbian, does she expect me to be a woman? I don't like having the only dick in the partnership. In a threesome, all these considerations disappear. I inhabit a special place between male and female and that's exactly where I like to be... as often as possible.

Out of the Darkness
Jakob Hero

When I was in high school I was desperate to know gay men. I sought them out in the place I had always heard they would be—the theater. Throughout my teen years I volunteered as a stagehand and an usher in a small black-box community theater. I found a lot of joy in that theater but the most important thing was being in close proximity to so many gay men. I emulated them. I patterned my clothes and my behaviors after theirs. I got to know them even though they didn't really take the time to know me. I was a depressed teenager with terribly low self-esteem. High school was a time when I felt like I was dying and many of the men I surrounded myself with actually were. This was the mid-1990s, before the AIDS cocktails of today, before protease-inhibitors. Many of these men were sick, some weren't, but what they all had in common was that they had become my heroes. I was 15 and had braces. I walked with the slouch of a person suffocating with self-loathing. But worst of all, I was a girl.

I would go home from the shows on Friday and Saturday nights, it would be late and I would feel so empty. I knew, or at least believed, that the guys were out partying. Sometimes I pretended the only reason they didn't invite me was that I was too young to go to nightclubs, but I knew it wasn't true. The reality of the situation was that they didn't invite me because I was invisible. I was just a girl.

Even knowing that I could never really belong there, I went back every weekend. That theater became my world. I was overwhelmed with adrenaline and excitement on those nights. When I got home I would be unable to sleep. I would sit up for most of the night replaying the conversations I had had with these men. Sometimes I would feel embarrassed, worrying that maybe at some point I had said the wrong thing, not realizing that it didn't matter since they would not remember anyway. I turned my anxiety into self-destruction. I would obsess about every moment at the theater as I later sat alone in my room, taking a razor blade to my shoulders, my tits, and the insides of my thighs. Whenever I was back in the theater I would be able to feel the cuts hidden under my clothes and I would wonder why I had done it, only to go home and repeat the whole ritual again and again.

Volunteering at the theater wasn't always a bad thing. In fact, it gave my life a meaning that I could not have found elsewhere. I have many memories of totally joyous moments when these guys paid attention to me. There were even many times when I made them laugh. Often I actually felt they liked me, even wanted me there, but those moments were never enough. I always left even emptier than I had been before I arrived. It seemed as if the life I lived around those gay men held up a magnifying glass to my complicated yet mundane existence as a teenage girl.

The emptiness grew from a place of deprivation, I always wanted more. I bled over it, hiding the physical wounds. Cutting myself was not a cry for attention. It was a source of great shame. I was always terrified that someone might find out. All I wanted was for them to like me, to see me as a protégé, to kid with me as if I were their little brother. I wanted an intimacy with them that was simply not possible. I used to imagine what they did with each other when I wasn't around, fantasies much bigger than the reality of their lives I now realize.

That was about twelve years ago. High school is long gone, as are my braces and breasts. Now I am a fag, too. I am no longer stuck in some crappy Southern town. I live in San Francisco. Of course, nothing is as simple as it sounds but the attention factor is no longer an issue. For one thing, I am no longer in such desperate need. I get attention from other gay men, and lots of it. Here in a city where youth is beauty I'm blessed, like many other FTMs, with looking significantly younger than my actual age. People here often assume I am just out of high school and fresh off the tractor from some godforsaken town, newly out, and totally in need of corruption.

Since I started my transition, years before moving here, I have been dating men which is something I didn't do as a girl. From my first interactions with gay men I have had to hold, comfort, and reassure them while they go through total crises about my body. For the first few years after transition I was very open to them and to their struggles but eventually it took its toll. I always try to be an open and compassionate person. I try to be supportive and loving. Sometimes I just wish that the amount of care-taking and support I give out would come back to me. How many times do I have to lovingly reassure guys whose hard-ons disappear when my underwear hits the floor? I let it get to me the first time, the fifth time, probably even the twentieth time that a fag came to me with a personal crisis over wanting to have sex. I wished my body were "normal." I let their fears, their closed-mindedness, their fucked-up cunt phobias make me feel worthless.

At some point I had to acknowledge that there are reasons I haven't had genital surgery. I actually like the parts I have and, beyond the fact that genital surgery is too expensive, I don't feel like I have to do that in order to be whole, no matter what other men have to say about my body. I can pinpoint the moment when I took the deficiency from myself and understood that I could no longer own other people's shame about my pussy. It wasn't fun or easy but I am grateful to the man who pushed me over that edge and towards some amount of newfound self-worth.

I met Andrej when I was living in Eastern Europe working in the field of LGBT human rights. I spent two years there fighting for the rights of queer people but rarely ever got to go home with any of them. I was in Ljubljana, Slovenia, one summer helping restore a gay community center and also helping to organize an LGBT Pride parade. It was there that I courted Andrej, a really hot Croatian man, for a couple of weeks. When finally I ended up in his bed, still fully clothed, he lost the courage (and with that the physical ability) to go through with it. I had fallen for him so hard that when he turned his own impotency into my issue I totally took that on. I felt disgusting. And when he told me that he believed he could love me if only I were different, I owned that, too. And lastly, as he cried and said he wished I would go away, have surgery, and then come back to him so we could be together, I held him. I stayed there and held him all night long. I felt sick and dirty. Throughout the night, when touching him was too painful for me I would try to pull away. But my resistance only made him hold me tighter and mumble in his sleep, "Please, Jakob, don't go."

Even if I wanted to leave, I couldn't. There were no trains to Zagreb, where I was living, until the next day. And that next day was terrible. I wanted to die. The two-hour train ride back to Zagreb was hell. I just didn't want to exist anymore. I felt broken, unlovable, dirty. One man's soft dick had become a burden that cast its shadow on my entire life. What should have been his embarrassment became my shame. With absolutely no sense of irony, I believed that he could have loved me if only I weren't who I am. I let that torture me for weeks. And then one day, I was done. Andrej was not the first, and certainly not the last, man to say those words to me. But, thankfully, he was the last one who got to take a piece of my soul away when he did.

And just as my teen years had eventually come to an end, so did my time overseas. When I first moved to San Francisco, I met a guy named Christopher. I liked him because he reminded me of one of those fags from back in my theater days who coincidentally had the same name. I loved to flirt with him. He was not really my type but was cute and fun to be around. Mostly my little crush was not based on an actual desire to hook up but rather a memory from when I was a girl who would have given anything to have a friend like Christopher. At some point, I don't really know when, Christopher found out that I am trans and started experiencing severe internal conflict about it and the feelings that he had for me. To him, this internal conflict was shocking. His fear about the meaning of his attraction to someone who used to be a girl was a new thing. But to me it was totally familiar, and to be honest, totally boring.

Of course, as he dealt with these feelings eventually he could no longer do so without bringing me into it. Christopher approached me recently and asked whether I had "gone all the way" and whether I had "had *the operation*." He asked this as if his question were so unique and strange that perhaps he was the first person ever to ask. I think he expected me to be surprised and maybe even offended. In actuality, his question was not the least bit unique. I knew where that conversation was headed from the moment he said, "There's something I really need to ask you..." I told him that I didn't mind answering his questions as long as he was willing to tell me what his motivation was in asking. I then explained to him that, yes, I have had all the surgery I plan to have. I am fully transitioned but, no, I have not had genital surgery. His disappointment was impossible to hide. He then said his motivation was just curiosity, nothing more.

Not long after that, I was talking to Christopher and some of our mutual friends. I said something about the town where I grew up. He told me he had lived there, too, for a few years, in the mid-1990s. I looked at him and I knew that he didn't just remind me of a Christopher I knew when I was a kid. This was him. And I was no longer invisible. I felt the blood drain from my face and with a weakness in my voice I asked him if he had been involved in community theater. I had learned to steel myself against morbid curiosities, against rejections, against horribly cruel remarks about my body, but something about realizing that someone in this new life of mine had known me *before* was just too much. Luckily, he probably never did know my name back then, he certainly can't remember what I looked like. His total lack of memory of the uncomfortable and awkward girl I once was is a total blessing. But even with him not being able to remember, just having this encounter with someone from my past felt like I had crashed my own party.

Suddenly there I was. I felt out of place. And I was slouching. It was like my wounds opened up. Blood rushed from each one of them, pulling my life force out of me. *What is that girl doing here?* I wondered about myself, just as they had wondered about me. *Why is she here? This is our space. This is our thing.* But there I was. Uncomfortable. Miserable. Bleeding. The old me invaded this place and forced me to recall the emptiness that had been my life. I was reminded of hopelessly longing to be exactly what I am today, not knowing that it would one day be possible. I think I had forgotten that girl. I had become invisible even to myself. The truth is that I barely survived my girlhood. And today, in a tight white t-shirt, black leather vest, and Levi's that hug my butt in just the right way, I have a secret doubt that I ever did escape being that girl.

However, much larger than the doubt I sometimes feel, is a clear feeling of triumph. So later on when Christopher came to me and said that he wasn't just curious about my surgeries for curiosity's sake, I was ready. He presented his dilemma as if his feelings were totally unique, as if he were the first person to ever be confronted with confusion about wanting what he had always despised. He told me that if only I were different he could feel comfortable liking me. Instead of owning that pain, I took a different route. I did not hold Christopher and comfort him while hearing that I am wretched. My pussy does not have to represent the shame and self-hatred of my past. I have worked really hard to get past my own trauma and I certainly don't need to live in someone else's. My cunt is not the embodiment of the horrible sexual encounter some fag had with a girl after his high school prom. I don't have to own this anymore. As if it was a palpable thing, I was able to take that shame Christopher had laid on me and, in my mind, roll it into a ball and place it into his hands. The truth is I also wish that things were different but I finally believe that the change that needs to happen is not in me. My body is not at fault here. And his disgust with what he fears he might find in my 501s is his shame, not mine. And while I will always hold potential sex partners and friends in respect, trust, and even love, I won't hold them through the night anymore while they shove me into the darkness. As clichéd as it might sound, I honor the path that got me here. I earned that right with my own blood. I have the scars, the battle wounds, to prove it. Most importantly, the girl I used to be doesn't have to be invisible to the fag I am today. I don't hate her, not her anxiety, not her braces, not even her tits. I have lived through torture, through what I have done and said to this body, and through what others have done and said to me. This scarred body is no longer an altar of pain and misery.

Thankfully, for every ten men like Andrej and Christopher, there are at least one or two who come along and are really comfortable and pleased with who and what I am. And that's great. In fact, it isn't a bad average. I have learned that this body can bring a lot of pleasure, for myself and for others. I am not that helpless kid anymore. After 27 years on this planet, I am ready for it to be okay for me to be who I am. San Francisco is a city of refugees. Here there are thousands of fags who, just like me, sought this place out with a desire to find safety in their own bodies. Finally, I am no different than them.

Fat, Trans and Single:
Some Thoughts from an "Othered" Body
on Control, Alienation, and Liberation
Joelle Ruby Ryan

One year ago, I was unceremoniously dumped. After close to four years, my then-partner, an FTM, told me that I did not fulfill his needs and that he was leaving the relationship. I was completely floored. I thought the relationship was skipping along just dandily but I was gravely mistaken. We stopped sleeping together that night. He started couch-surfing with friends and moved out altogether a few months later, eventually taking up residence with his new lover. One of my worst fears was realized once again: I was alone.

For most of my life I have been single. Part of this has been due to how difficult it is to find partners when you inhabit a multiply "othered" body. I am 6'6" tall and over 350 pounds. I am also a "no-ho, no-op" transgender person, which means that I have opted not to take hormones or pursue surgical intervention although I support these medical options for those who choose or need them. Living as an openly fat, tall, queer, trans person, and trying mightily to be proud of all of these things, has proven to be an extreme challenge and one that has unfortunately had a negative effect on my dating life.

Although the genderqueer movement has made impressive strides in promoting acceptance of all bodies and identities, the trans movement often has problems accepting people whose identities fall between or outside the gender binary, as well as with acknowledging and celebrating trans bodies of size. For some, physical and/or medical transition fits like a glove, with new roles as women or men feeling incredibly comfortable, genuine and safe. Sometimes I experience jealousy when I see transexuals settle into a state of "gender euphoria" in their desired roles because, for some of us, the search for identity continues unabated. We are constantly in transition, trying to negotiate our gender identities and expressions in a societal structure which has no place, no words, and no affirmations for our very lives.

I am not a man and I am not a woman. Yet people almost always place me in one category or the other. My parents have never accepted my trans-ness and view me eternally as their son. They call me "he" and use my birth name when communicating. Many friends, with much more liberal and compassionate intentions, react with anger when someone calls me "he" as if my "womanhood" needs some kind of defense. Often I want to scream, "It doesn't matter! You're both wrong. I am neither a man nor a woman."

My parents reacted to my fatness the same way they reacted to my trans-ness. When I came out of the transgender closet, they wanted me to seek help and try to change into a normal heterosexual man. My father had hopes that working with the right counselor would cure me and set me on the path of the straight and narrow. As I gained weight over the years, my parents commented on my size and goaded me to go on diets, exercise, and try to lose weight. If I tried hard enough, I could shed the pounds, live a healthier life, and look better.

What do these things have in common? The body in American culture is constantly being controlled by our families, medical establishment, media, government, church, and multiple other socio-cultural institutions. Bodies that don't conform need to be fixed. Intersex babies born with non-standard genitalia, chromosomal patterns, or secondary sex characteristics need to be "repaired" by surgeons and endocrinologists. Gender-variant children need to be "cured" by notorious doctors such as Kenneth Zucker to conform to strict notions of masculinity and femininity. Fat people need to have weight-loss surgery to better conform to hegemonic ideals of body size. Today, tall pre-teen natal females are being given estrogen to halt growth while boys with "idiopathic shortness" are given human growth hormone to become taller. Despite an incredibly diverse population, those in positions of power push a mythical norm of size and gender that privileges heterosexuality, gender normativity, thinness, and an average or slightly tall height.

All my life I have been asked, "How tall are you? Are you a boy or a girl?" More recently, I am asked how much I weigh, whether I am on a diet, and do I know that excess weight is unhealthy. At a recent trans convention, I went to a function that had a line of hors d'oeuvres. When

I started to fill my plate, the trans woman beside me gave me a look to kill and started to comment before my angry grimace made her stop. This scenario ruined the event and reminded me how much fatphobia there is in all sectors of society, including my own community. For any person, it is an uphill battle to develop a sense of self-esteem when you're constantly told that you are not good enough. But fat genderqueer and trans people face special barriers because we are in the throes of a so-called "obesity epidemic" compounded by profound hatred for sexual ambiguities of any kind. Often I think, *Whose body is it, anyways?* From birth, we are taught the importance of "being yourself" and taking ownership of your life. When some of us take that ownership, society shits all over us.

When I participate in transgender panels at universities, people are itching to talk about sexuality. While the panelists are there to talk about gender identity, gender expression, and the social construction of gender in American culture, students want to know who we are doing it with, and how, and why. Many times I have had a student ask, "Are you attracted to guys or girls?" I stammer with an answer because the question itself is deeply flawed.

First of all, I don't consider myself a man or a woman. The sexual (dis)orientation system is based upon the notion that one has a stable, coherent identity as a man or a woman. Second, the question presumes that there are only two choices (men and women) to whom one could be attracted. My world view is that there are multiple genders and that they all are attractive in different and similar ways. Third, the question erases asexuality (lack of sexual attraction) and bisexuality/pansexuality (attraction to more than one gender / resistance to monosexuality). I am not trying to demonize those who ask. Undoubtedly, they are motivated by curiosity and lack of knowledge about trans people's sexualities. Society places limits on sexuality just as it does on gender, body shape and size. I now identify as asexual, queer, and pansexual to call attention to the fluidity and constantly evolving nature of sexuality and eroticism, or lack thereof.

Having the body that I do, not to mention the complex identities, makes finding accepting partners very challenging. I often feel like my body and identity are unintelligible in our society. My gender, size, and sexuality place me in uncharted territory. "Are you gay or straight?" has become like a broken record. "None of the above!" I want to scream.

In addition, compulsory pair-bonding is also very much a strict cultural requirement. Celibate people, single people, non-monogamous people, and polyamorous folks continue to be stigmatized for failing to conform to hegemonic notions of monogamous, married coupledom. Sadly, the focus on gay marriage, while admirable in some respects, has helped to further emphasize marriage, monogamy, and couplehood. While all people, regardless of gender, should be able to enter into legal marriage contracts, the movement is based on an assimilationist model. Alternative forms of dating, sexuality, and domestic arrangements have been heavily stigmatized in the quest for this emerging "homo-normativity." When you are single, it can be very difficult to maintain a healthy sense of identity when all around you are bombarded with images of happy, smiling couples as the hegemonic norm. Often single people are made to feel like failures, made to feel that we can never be happy, and told that there is something wrong with us because we have not been able to find and keep a long-term partner.

Would I prefer to have a loving intimate partner? Absolutely! My relationship with my ex gave me many wonderful things and a future relationship could do the same. I am open to it and sincerely hope that it happens. However, I also must find ways to nurture my soul while finding contentment in the here and now, and that means being single. End the social rhetoric and the negative self-talk that we are somehow "less than" because we are not partnered. In fact, there are advantages to being single and many opportunities for self-growth and self-exploration. We must constantly affirm ourselves and say, "We are fine just the way we are."

The kind of hateful backlash that has been heaped upon Thomas Beatie, the "pregnant man," is absolutely appalling. Beatie is a path-breaker and a very brave person to come forward with his experience. If we are going to talk about the fluidity of sex, gender, sexuality, and reproduction, then we truly have to support all of its diverse manifestations. I was irate that Beatie had received such a lukewarm response from some members of the trans community. Many trans people, like their cisgender counterparts, reacted to Thomas Beatie's pregnancy with fear. They worried that he was going to make it worse for us because his actions are so "out there." Well, guess what gender-normative gay people have been saying about trans people for decades? Rather than shun Beatie, we should embrace him and see him as a pioneer who is expanding the choices and options for all of us. No, he is certainly isn't the first pregnant FTM. I understand some question his desire for the media spotlight but that doesn't change the many good things that will come out of his story. I love and respect people who push the envelope, and it is particularly pivotal in this time of dreadful cultural conservatism. Breaking free from the status quo mold will enable us to be better and go further, dreaming of possibilities that our queer and trans ancestors could never have imagined.

Those of us who inhabit "othered" bodies and identities—queer, fat, short, tall, trans, intersex, disabled, pierced, tattooed, single, asexual, poly, in some way considered "freaky" or unintelligible to mainstream culture—have in our possession a double-edged sword. On one hand, we suffer mightily from cultural oppression. There is a lifetime of wounds inflicted by our families, our churches, schools, and peer groups. Being so different has opened me up to tremendous loneliness, isolation, and alienation. As a kid and adolescent, I would escape into the world of books to discover parallel universes that were more accepting and fulfilling. Until several years ago, I would always leave the house with my headphones on blasting music, both to block out literally the drive-by voices of the oppressors and to keep anyone at bay because people hurt me so damn much. To this day, I struggle with social phobia and with keeping in touch with people. Sometimes it just seems easier not to try (and not be hurt) then to face rejection and rebuffing. Sometimes the loneliness causes great depression and I struggle to find a way to be joyful in this world that systematically erases me, negates my identities, and tells me I am inferior. My fellow outlaws suffer similarly and I often rage against a world that engenders so much pain and anguish.

But within every body outlaw lies the spirit of a formidable warrior. We did not get this far by accident. Within the deepest recesses of our beings, there blazes a fire that can never be extinguished. From the Tenderloin to Stonewall, the intensity of my queer/trans ancestors pushes me onward, all the while saying that nothing is impossible. For all the hardship, adversity, and pain, I would not change who I am for anything. Ever. Now, this is not to say that I am a martyr. Would I change the societal conditions that foster oppression? Hell, yes! I and countless activists and social change agents are working mightily to do just that. But being who I am has required me to fight, has given me a critical mindset to challenge all of the bullshit. Being who I am has made me think about oppressions like racism and Islamophobia that I do not face because I can see how all forms of domination are interconnected.

The great poet Essex Hemphill in his poem "In the Life" addresses his mother and tells her that despite the many hardships he has faced in life as a Black, gay man, he is proud and happy of the life he has chosen. "Do not feel shame for how I live. I chose this tribe of warriors and outlaws." When we are put down, we must hold each other up. We must work tirelessly to celebrate all of society's outcasts and demand our inherent equality and humanity. Use the life we are given to provoke change and foster love in all its myriad forms. My greatest hope is to see diverse people come together to fight for a radically different world. I believe it is both within our reach and within our lifetime. Audre Lorde often said some variation of the following statement to people she met: "I am a Black, lesbian, feminist, socialist, mother, poet, warrior, doing my work. Are you doing yours?" To paraphrase Lorde's brilliance, I would say: I am a fat, single, genderqueer, transfeminist, writer, teacher, activist, trying very hard to do my work. Are you doing yours? And can we work together to transform the world and fight the good fight?

Shifting Sexuality or How I Learned to Stop Worrying and Be a Bisexual Tranny Dyke
Ashley Altadonna

The night I tearfully called my mother and told her I was transgendered, she reassured me that she loved me no matter what but couldn't help asking, "Are you sure you're not just gay?" I gave a much relieved laugh and told her, "Yes, I'm sure." Later, when I asked why she thought I might be gay, she explained that she had always wondered since the time I was in high school when she threw out my "favorite" shirt.

In high school I was a teenage suburban grunge rocker, sadly seven years too late. I was the epitome of pathetic imitation in my ripped jeans, long hair, and a dirty wool cardigan. So the fact that I wore a tightly fitted, polyester, buttoned-up, collared shirt that I found at a thrift store must have struck my mom as "special" in contrast to the array of baggy flannel that usually made up my wardrobe. One afternoon in art class, I accidentally got a tiny smudge of yellow ochre oil paint on the left sleeve. If you've ever tried to get oil paint out of clothes, you know there's no point. It didn't bother me but it must have driven my mom crazy because she decided to throw the shirt away.

I was taking out the trash when I noticed my shirt lying there discarded amongst the garbage bags. Like any self-righteous teenager, I stormed back inside and demanded to know why my shirt had become refuse. My mother pointed out the stain with a look of disbelief. I yelled at her never to throw my things away again without asking me first! This incident somehow made the shirt my favorite, just as its tight fit and polyester blend somehow made me gay.

As ridiculous as this sounds as a justification for my supposed homosexuality, my mother is far from being prejudiced against gay people. Rather she was simply uninformed about trans people. In fact, the question of whether or not I was gay was one I had asked myself when coming to terms with my transexualism. I often thought it would be easier if I were "simply gay." Gay people, in general, aren't inclined to buy entirely new wardrobes, make-up, electrolysis, or voice lessons in order to be seen as male or female. Homosexual men and women don't generally need to receive recommendations from licensed therapists in order to obtain costly hormone therapies or expensive surgeries to align their bodies and minds. This is due to the fact that homosexuality has been removed from the DSM (Diagnostic and Statistical Manual of Mental Disorders) while transgender identity disorder remains a mental illness. Of course, there's the debate of whether removing it would hinder trans folks from receiving medical treatments since most insurance companies still consider the needs of transgender people to be unworthy of coverage.

Likewise, people who are "simply gay" aren't often required to get court orders and change their names or birth certificates to have their genders recognized legally. Gay men and lesbians lack many of the rights bestowed upon straight society but, at the very least, they're usually still considered men and women!

When I lived as a man, I considered myself straight. I only dated women. It wasn't that I was opposed to the idea of dating men but I was never really attracted to them physically. In my early twenties, I dated quite a few women and the subject of my transexualism was something that I kept hidden from nearly all of them. I was twenty-five when I met my girlfriend, Maria, at a bar one night through mutual friends. We bonded over cheap drinks and third-wave feminist ideals. Maria and I had been dating for a few months before I managed to work up the courage to tell her I was transgender. At the time, I considered my transexualism more of a cross-dressing fetish, and I was deeply ashamed and embarrassed by it. To my surprise, Maria was supportive and open-minded. We talked and decided to take the "girl thing" very slow.

Eventually, Maria asked if she could see me dressed as a girl. I was extremely nervous but I desperately wanted to be able to share the side of me that I had kept concealed for so long. We set a date for her to come over to my apartment and I would be dressed up. That whole day I was sick with nervous excitement. I shaved my legs and face, and did my make-up. I tried my best to be as natural and feminine as possible. I'm sure I looked like a mess but Maria was so wonderful. She told me I was beautiful and she made me feel that way, too. On our six-month anniversary, we went to the beach and she gave me her silver heart necklace. She said that I was the bravest, sweetest person she knew. Needless to say, my heart melted.

Maria gave me the courage to transition. She was there with me as I made my initial public appearances "en femme." I was terrified the first time we went to the grocery store with me as a female. I insisted we go to a store across town just to be sure that no one would recognize me. She was by my side as my constant source of strength as we made our way from aisle to aisle. She repeatedly told me I was gorgeous when I didn't want to believe I was anything more than some sort of horrible freak.

Many people asked if Maria and I planned to stay together, as if a trans woman and cisgendered woman were somehow incompatible. When we told them we would, they inevitably asked, "What does that make you then, lesbians?" We would smile and nod. When one partner is transgender, it calls into question all those labels we put on relationships. How a couple chooses to define their relationship varies as widely as each couple does. Maria and I were excited about embracing our newfound queer identities. However, it was a definite adjustment going from being a straight couple to a queer one.

Suddenly becoming a member of a minority, straight culture seemed to be everywhere. It was a little overwhelming to stand outside the heterosexual matrix and look in. Once people started perceiving me as female, there was the concern of how affectionate we ought to be in public or amongst our families. This was something we never thought about when we were perceived as straight. There was a period early on where I was self-conscious about even holding hands. I didn't care so much if people read us as dykes but rather that the attention would cause someone to read me as trans.

Next, people always asked the ridiculous question of who played what role in the relationship. People assumed that, even though we were now queer, we must automatically model our relationship on a heterosexual context. This did bring up the complex issue of gender roles in our relationship. We had always strived for equality as a couple and those cultural stereotypes of "what a man or woman should be" didn't quite apply. Now that I was female, would it be assumed that Maria would still be the one to cook and clean? Who would be the one to change car tires or pay when we were out? While most of these issues worked themselves out on their own, it was interesting to note the differences that my transition brought about. For instance, Maria has told me she was caught off-guard the first time I used the same public bathroom as her when we were at a dance club. This last place of solitude from one's partner was suddenly gone.

Many people assumed that as I transitioned my sexuality would change, too. For better or worse, they were right! It seemed to happen all at once. I began to notice a sudden need for male attention. This came as a shock since it was something I hadn't experienced before or expected to happen. It was as if a switch was flipped and I started finding men attractive. I would catch myself staring at some guy longer than I would have before. Male customers started acting a whole lot friendlier at the bookstore where I work. I began to wonder if the hot boy browsing the art books would notice me. Some of my change in thinking about men came from not only being allowed culturally, but also from the expectation that as a woman I ought to find men attractive. There also became a clear distinction that I was no longer "one of the guys." As a woman, men began to talk over me or exclude me from conversations I would have normally been included in. While the sisterhood of women opened up to me, the brotherhood of men closed. There was suddenly this notion of "us and them." It became more and more difficult to communicate with the men in my life, like my father and brother. This exclusion or separation was a part of what made male attention suddenly seem desirable.

Sometimes male attention was given but not necessarily wanted, like one time at a friend's Halloween party where I went dressed as a witch. The hat I bought for the costume unfortunately didn't fit. People weren't sure if I was a "real" girl or some dude in drag. Two frat boys were debating the topic right in front of me. I was about to tell them they could simply ask, when one of them grabbed my tits! I hadn't experienced this sort of blatant objectification before and it was a definite shock. There was also the time some creep cornered me as I was waiting at a deserted bus stop and asked me if he could fuck me up the ass! Without warning, I had become a target for male sexist oppression.

There have been good moments, too. Like the times a cute boy calls me "pretty" or "sexy," and when some halfway-decent guy asks me out (though I inevitably tell him I'm taken). Or when a good-looking man opens the door or buys me a drink. In those moments, I get butterflies in my stomach. Some of this is definitely the thrill of being gendered correctly as female and receiving validation that I am considered passable, if not beautiful. But sometimes it goes beyond that. I've begun to fantasize what it would be like to date a guy, and when my transwomen friends tell me of their experiences with men, I get slightly jealous. Or worst of all, when Maria and I are having sex, it's so good but I can literally feel the vagina I don't yet have. I want to be penetrated and start to wonder if sex might be better with a man. All these things build up and I feel guilty because I know what I have with Maria is so amazing. Recently, the stress of all this guilt has landed me back in therapy. In figuring out my bisexuality, I began questioning what I wanted from my relationship with Maria. Maybe things would be easier if I was with a man. It could clear up the question of those pesky gender roles. I would be the sole female in the relationship and this, in turn, might help me feel more secure in my femininity. Was I missing out on some important aspect of womanhood by not being involved with a man? All these unknowns kept plaguing me. Maria began to worry that I wanted to leave her for a guy. I felt terrible for hurting her but I wasn't even sure what I wanted myself. This went on for a week or two. We started to argue about what I should do. Though we had often talked about the possibility of me liking men, it was always a "we'll cross that bridge when we come to it" situation. All at once, we were there.

Finally, I couldn't take the stress anymore and had a major nervous breakdown. I felt like everything was falling apart and it was all my fault. I couldn't sleep and I cried buckets and buckets worth of tears. I had to leave work early one day because I couldn't handle worrying about it anymore. I called Maria and told her I had left work. She begged me to come back home. Emotionally exhausted, I went back. Once again, Maria saved me. She said she forgave me, and understood I wasn't intending to hurt her. Once the breakdown was over, it was a major relief. The weight from the past three years was finally lifted. It was as if I had cried out all the guilt, worry, and frustration.

Maria and I are dealing with my shifting sexuality. I'm more confident than ever in the future of our relationship. Whether I'm attracted to girls or boys doesn't stress me out like it did before. She makes me happy and that's all that truly matters. Coming to terms with my sexuality has been almost as difficult as coming to terms with my gender but thanks to my girlfriend at least I know I'm not alone.

Milk, please!
This is how my days go. The boys always remember to say "please." Manners are important to their Ma and me. I am Papa in my house and my days are punctuated with little boys yelling for me from the kitchen or crawling into my lap to tell me a story. I am a domestic man teaching my sons to follow suit. They love to clean and put clothes into the washer, they think I'm amazing when I steam-vac the floors. I keep asking myself if I am teaching them all the things they need to know as boys to survive out there when it is time. When fatherhood came, it hit like a volcano sitting dormant. I wasn't expecting to fall in love with that first view of the monitor. It wasn't easy. I wasn't ready. I had just figured out how to be this man and now I was taking on a whole new role.

Hurrah!
This is the moment we cheer. My 3-year-olds are potty-trained and every time someone makes it to the potty there is an instant celebration. This reminds me of the medical steps I took to achieve this body, how my partner was my cheerleader. When she calls me her beautiful man the trumpets sound in my chest. Before her, I never liked myself enough to know what it meant to be loved. It sounds clichéd, I know, but I believe it to be true.

My sons make me evaluate over and over the label of "man," make me redefine what it is to be beautiful. When I think about achievements like walking, teething, and potty-training, I remember the way we clapped and said, "Good job!" I keep reminding myself this kind of praise shouldn't end.

When I was a kid there was never a "Good job!" rolling off the lips of my parents. I worked hard to please and usually my best was far from good enough for them. My father was usually absent and my real father had died a long time ago. I had a brother who couldn't do the things with me that I wanted to do so I depended on the bikers, farmers, and construction workers whom I grew up around. My masculinity comes from men in the fields, beers around bonfires, and chopping wood. Where I live now, there are no fields or bonfires and I have no need for chopped wood. From these men I learned that being a man was a broken back and drinking. Most of them were in marriages they hated and with kids like me who had no promise of making it past gravel roads. They took solace in those cold beers, in those brown bottles. The night air always smelled thick with whiskey. What I learned from the men around me was that, as a girl, none of those men were gonna love me, and that I may end up with a woman who wouldn't appreciate me. These were their stories and I didn't want them to be mine. What stands out in all of that, though, is the level of commitment those guys had.

Check yes or no!

My real father worked double-shifts at the shipyard and my adoptive father jumped off trains. When he wasn't jumping off trains, we baked: he secretly dreamed of being a pastry chef. The boys and I bake at least once a week and we cook together often. I think of my dad in these times and I wonder if he would appreciate the man I've become. These days I think of him as the guy who bought me. I wonder if at some point my kids will believe me to be the guy who bought the other half of their DNA.

There is not always happiness in fatherhood. There are broken bones and scraped knees and the flu; there is bedtime and time-outs and tantrums. Before these things, we had the NICU (neo-natal intensive care unit). I wondered if the nurse could tell I was a different kind of man. After tubes and bilirubin lights for jaundice, after apnea and incubators, I had the moments I had dreamed about: my boys and I, bare chests to bare chest. Other transmen called me stupid for wanting kids, for staying in a long-term relationship. They told me I would never really be a father, that other men would not look me in the eye when I was out with my boys. As men, we are taught to be providers and nothing more. I am a provider. When they say "provider," they mean "bringin' home the bacon," making enough money to take care of the wife and children. The idea that I don't provide for my family is laughable to any stay-at-home parent. I am the maid, cook, preschool teacher. I am the launderer, handyman, nurse... I am what they would consider to be a "renaissance man" if anyone actually valued all of my skills.

I'm scared!

I want to tell them, "You should be," but I know better. Right now they are scared of the dark or being up too high in a play structure. Nobody told me I should be afraid. I came into this world chest first and that's the way I've approached it ever since. I ran into transition like a kid runs towards an ice cream truck. I didn't know that as a transman I would become an individual some people fear.

I am not a big man, that's not what makes me scary. It's my skin. Before 9/11, I was a hoodlum. After 9/11, I was a terrorist. Either way, I'm some sort of pain in the ass. I became a stain in a sea of white men in my own community, I am a token. Before I stuck that needle to flesh, before I cut off parts of my body, I was just a girl nobody noticed. I was oversized clothes and dirty sneakers blending into the vinyl of a bus seat. Now I am still dirty sneakers but blending is a thing of the past. Cops follow me home, pull me over for something to do. Airport security makes me physically ill for a week before my trip. Somehow my presence makes the world stop running smoothly, throws a wrench into someone's otherwise perfect day. When I'm doing yard work, I'm the hired help. When I'm out with my kids, I'm the nanny. When my partner and I are out at community functions, I'd like to remind folks that we have a right to be there. It's an age-old battle of proving queerness: I would like to be invited to queer parenting groups where I don't have to discuss my genitals or our sperm donor... who is just that: a sperm donor. We don't know him.

We don't play guns in my house. There is no play-fighting or wrestling. When people question my intentions, they tell me these things are just harmless games, but war is real, guns are real, death happens every day. If the world suspects me of being a terrorist, I wonder how they will view my children. They are, after all, mixed blood though one is blonde-haired with blue eyes and his skin is pale, while the other is olive-complexioned with hazel eyes and sandy hair. I worry for the day they defend their ethnicity; I worry for the day they start defending us as their parents. I want to arm them with words and witty retorts, not fists. So instead we play dress up, make music, color. We swing from the monkey bars, ride bikes, splash in the tub. I want to keep these times in boxes on the shelf as a reminder of masculinity for my sons.

I'm often asked if I'm more aware as a father because I am a transman. People think as a former woman I am a better parent, they believe the way I nurture these boys has something to do with being raised a girl. If I could introduce you to my mothers, you would think twice about the idea that all women are soft. I learned gentleness from my fathers. My quick short answer to those questions is usually "I don't think so." I wasn't much of a girl. When you grow up in a small town, out in the sticks where work needs to be done, gender isn't much of an excuse for not getting dirty. In fact, most of my growing up was genderless until the moments when a dress was laid out on my bed, or when puberty hit and they didn't sell any sort of masculine bras or tampons for those hitting female puberty.

There are days I don't like my body, days I don't want to think about how my kids might one day grow to hate me. I worry that even though I am their Papa they will want to know their donor. I wake up in sweats worrying my wife will die and I will lose the best thing we have ever done, that someone will take my kids, question my paternity. I worry that in one foul motion because of this body, because of this medical problem, because of this thing I consider a disorder, I will lose everything. I want to say to my boys, "Be scared, you should be," but I have hope that they will hold their own against a world that promises to scare them.

Again? Yes, please!

We are doing it again. By "it," I mean we are having more kids. This is like going to graduate school: you know the work expected to make the grade but it gets harder the more kids you add to a house. This time I am less stressed. I don't care who thinks I should or shouldn't be having kids. I am no longer second-guessing my masculinity because my hands aren't calloused like they used to be. I am a family man. I like bouncing on beds, Saturday morning cartoons, and making excuses to have chocolate cake for breakfast. I like the way my lady cradles her belly while she creates some of the most healing people I will ever meet. It's as if the internal rhyme of her is telling these babies to save my life. Before I became Papa I was just a guy looking for some reason to cling to life like it was a good thing. We are told as trans folks/queers that we don't deserve the right to get married and have families. Some of our own throw stones and when my choices are being protested, I hear that I don't deserve the right to love. I love myself enough to be this man. I love myself enough to fall for someone who fell for me. I love myself enough to teach my little ones how different love can look without any restraints. I think I did okay. I think we did okay.

City Hall
Phyllis Pseudonym

Cody's taking his time shaving. Since he's only been on hormones for a month or so, there isn't much hair to begin with. Nonetheless, he lathers, talks about that straight razor he wants so bad, and complains that it'll take weeks for what he does have to grow back. Charmed by his excitement and grateful that he's making an effort, I pat the small of his back and set to my own face with a toxic green, three-blade woman's razor.

In the kitchen our coffee contentedly gurgles and spits. I towel off, pour two cups, and liberally butter Cody's English muffins. Without thinking, I munch on one of them, staring out my window at Brooklyn. It's still half-dark and the commuters rub sleep from their eyes en route to the G train. Glancing at the wristwatch tacked above the stove, I note that it's already seven-thirty, and having drawn a bad time slot we're due at City Hall in an hour. "The blue hour," I'd giggled as we received our marriage license a couple of days earlier, "how romantic."

But romance is, at best, an indirect factor today. I do love Cody in ways I have never loved anybody else, and in spite of the way he's looking at his one-and-a-quarter English muffins, it's evident that the feeling is reciprocated. We share a futon mattress, household chores, the occasional pair of underwear, sex toys, and a lover or two. We are also planning to adopt a couple of dogs later this year.

But all of this is peripheral. My student visa is running short and since my transition the thought of returning home fills me with a terrible sense of nausea. About a year and a half ago, before he'd moved in, Cody showed sympathy and proposed that we just make a trip over to City Hall and get my green card taken care of. Much as the legal institution of marriage runs against my general political outlook, I wasn't about to turn down that kind of offer.

Come to think of it, as long as we had the papers and could stay living together, wouldn't it be sort of amusing to enshrine our little slice of queer domestic bliss in the language of a widespread, completely flawed but ultimately irrelevant concept of romance? Hell, we might even get a toaster oven or some bed linen out of my folks.

"A toaster oven?! Are you fuckin' listening to yourself?" The same afternoon Cody first suggested we do this, he made his feelings concerning the idea of marriage abundantly clear, rolling out of my bed and edging up against the wall to underscore his sense of horror and disgust. "I'm not signing on for a toaster oven! I don't want bed linen! And I'll say this just once: I am never going to be anybody's wife! This isn't going to be a marriage. It's nothing more than a legal contract that'll keep you in the country, okay?"

Shaking off a post-coital haze, I attempted to reason some calm back into the situation. "But wouldn't it be sort of a radical destabilization of the institution or something? Being married-unmarried, performing husband and wife, or wife and husband, or husband and husband, or whatever as the mood suited? I mean, it wouldn't have to mean anything more than what we settled on in the moment. Like, we could just turn it on or off. You couldn't pin us down!"

Cody, however, finds rather less humor in the potential ironies of this situation than do I. He grew up dirt poor in southern Iowa, the eldest child in a family rife with domestic violence, alcoholism, and homophobic blood-and-fire Christianity. Having never returned, his only connection to home is a twice yearly call from his grandmother: a roll call of teen pregnancies, methamphetamine busts, and Iraq casualties followed by inquiries as to whether her "little girl has found a nice husband to bring home and take care of us yet."

Though I do my best to show sensitivity and discretion, just about every discussion we've had on the matter for the last eighteen months has built into heated, then hysterical, arguments followed by crescendos of frantic make-up sex. I've learned to broach the subject obliquely and when I do it's not so much marriage as "marriage" accompanied by an airborne set of quotation marks.

"Whoa, have you seen the time?" Cody waves his cell phone at me. "We need to keep on task. I didn't wake up at six in the morning to roll in late!" It took us most of last night and quite a few whiskeys to work out our wedding attire. Cody's best attempt at straight soft-butch hangs up neatly in our wardrobe while my outfit lies in a heap on the floor beside the bed. I pick up a checked vintage cowboy shirt, brush it off, and pull it onto my back. Not standard matrimonial attire but since we cropped my hair short a week back it's kind of a look and, really, what better costume for an immigration marriage?

"A little help?" he requests. I glance up, walk down to Cody's side of the bed in my shirt and panties, and smooth out his lapel. He rolls his head back and stares down at me with the same macho satisfaction he shows every time we do this little ritual. I stop buttoning him halfway up, allowing a generous display of cleavage. He's wearing one of my bras, padded and a cup-and-a-half too small, and as he fastens one extra button I ponder how much I'll miss those creamy globes after he gets his surgery.

Hustling downstairs and into the cab, Cody slouches against the door, tosses a leg over my knee, and tells me to stop fussing over our damn documents. Unable to help myself, I unfold and inspect our marriage license. It's a poor photocopy, filled out in green ballpoint, and rubber-stamped with the New York state coat of arms. At the bottom of the form I can just barely make out a warning in capital letters against FOLDING, MUTILATING, OR FALSIFYING THIS DOCUMENT. I curse inwardly, smooth out the crease, and set the paper back into the manila folder with our other papers. Cody stares out the window at the Brooklyn Bridge and beyond to the Statue of Liberty.

"How're you doing? Tired?" I ask.

He looks back at me, offers an opaque smile. "Just fine, baby, just fine."

Out the window, cars roll up FDR Drive with resigned determination; a lone commuter ferry makes its way to where I do not know. As a child, I had fantasized about lavish outdoor wedding ceremonies in the midst of delicate snowfalls. My hair would be worn up like Jennifer Connelly in the opening scene of *Labyrinth* and my dress would be of elaborate white lace, with veils and a long train; my bride would wear a matching gown. Studying the dog-shit brown of late winter midtown, I'm struck by how much more fun snow was when I was eight years old and imagining it from the comfort of a Pacific island.

The cab sweeps off the bridge and dumps us out in front of the municipal building. We clamber over a mountain of ice the color of cigarette ash, cross the plaza, and enter through the side door reserved for non-employees. For all of City Hall's imposing external architecture, the side entrance through which we pass is remarkably shabby. The wainscoting has begun to warp in places, and a trace of mid-century cigarette smoke still lingers in the thick air. Inside it must be pushing ninety degrees and I immediately break into a profuse , uncomfortable sweat. Three security guards in long sleeves slouch around a metal detector discussing their plans for the weekend.

Pausing between bites of her bagel, one of the guards addresses the line, "Have your photo IDs ready, bags open, people!" The line shuffles forward, winter coats in arms. Nobody says anything.

"And what are we here for today?" the guard asks us. "We're here to get married. I have our IDs and our license—" Our guard glances at the documents, looks me over, scowls. "No, I think you got the wrong document. I think you want a civil union." Taken aback, I glance at my feet. Cody shoots daggers, the guard laughs out loud, throws our papers on the desk beside my bags, and shifts his attention to the line behind us. "Have your photo IDs ready. Bags open, people!"

The directory points us to a mezzanine elevator bank. We board and I point out that the elevator walls are covered with the same Formica as the F train. Cody turns and pulls me into focus for a moment but maintains a grim, vulnerable, macho silence. Inwardly forgiving his stoniness, I make a mental note to keep chatter to a minimum till we're out of here.

The elevator doors open onto a corridor filled with wedding parties and pandemonium. Ignoring the sign appealing for calm and quiet, people chatter and laugh with excitement all around us. Everywhere hands are held and arms thrown around waists and shoulders. A couple of teenage Polish elopers prevail upon the patriarch of a large, smartly dressed, Persian family to take a photo. A man in a tailored suit and wingtips with a woman in bright West African dress beam at one another in a doorway. People check their reflections in an interior window, fixing hair and makeup with little concern for the roomful of people working on the other side. There is no white lace in evidence. At the end of the hallway a security guard sets her crossword down, checks a clipboard, and calls over the hubbub, "Uh... Grazbowski-Wozniak? I got that right? Grabowski-Wozniak!"

The young Poles skip through the door beside her. We stew in our sweat for a quarter of an hour, during which time perhaps five wedding parties are called through. Cody adjusts his bra, closes his eyes, and shuffles his feet.

"Martin-Werner! Where is Martin-Werner?" We bundle up our coats, flash the marriage license, and she waves us through into the court. To our left, the officiant, wearing a blue button-down shirt and comfortable shoes stands behind a podium. Opposite her, the American flag and New York state flag hang from crossed poles. Straight ahead, an illuminated exit sign promises that the end is mercifully imminent. "Okay, so you're, uh, Heidi?" asks the officiant, looking at me. I shake my head no and nod at Cody, who is staring into space with all the guilty intensity of an eighth-grader about to receive a dressing down in the principal's office. This doesn't bode well for our interview with the Department of Homeland Security. But the reprimand never comes. Utterly unfazed by her mistake, the officiant motions for us to step up to the podium. I suppose, by the standards of City Hall, we're just two more in a very long line of freaks and weirdos.

"Did you bring your own vows, or you want a standard one?"

"Is it religious?" needles Cody, emboldened. "'Cause I'm pretty sure we're both already going to hell." Cool as a cucumber, she shuffles through a stack of papers on the podium, pulls one to the top and inhales deeply.

"Do you, MATHEWPHILIPEMARTIN, take HEIDIWAR-NER to be your lawfulyweddedwife, insicknessandinhealthtilldeathdoy-oupart?"

I glance at Cody and answer in the affirmative. He looks as bemused by this masterfully sterile delivery as I am glad for it, and as the officiant reads off the bride's portion of the script, he suddenly offers me a conspiratorial wink. He answers "Yep." She stares down her nose at him. He corrects his posture and adds, "I do."

"Then by the power vested in me by the stateoftheCityofNewYork, I now pronounce you husbandandwife. Your certificate should arrive in the mail within the next ten business days. Congratulations and have a nice day."

Recalling our lawyer's advice to collect as many photos as possible, I dig out the camera we borrowed from Cody's mother and ask the officiant to take a photo. She obliges and we solemnly pose in front of the flags with arms around one another. The flash fires and I ask for another. Turning to Cody, I whisper, "This one's for the Feds," and kiss him on the lips. He even lets me slip a little tongue and as we pull apart he smiles and sighs with relief.

We step out into the cold, crisp air through a back door, and navigating around a dumpster Cody quizzically glances back at the building. "Did she really say, 'The state of the city of New York'?" I giggle and give him a hug. "You're a fuckin' rock star. I promise I'll never make you do this ever again. Now, let's go get some eats."

Back in Brooklyn, President Bush is on the diner's TV making another impassioned and thoughtful case for preservation of the heterosexual family but I'm far more interested in conversation about the various tattoos Cody and I each want next. When the waitress arrives to take our plates, I down the remainder of my cup of coffee and ask if we could please possibly get one more top-up with our check? She waddles off and he pulls me further into the booth, planting a kiss on the nape of my neck. "You wanna go home and have a fuuuck?" Now that he's also on hormones, Cody has to have sex like five times a day, which is more than fine by me. "Uh-huuuuuh." But first thing I need to do when we get home is file away our papers and this marriage certificate where they belong, all together, in the file marked 'Immigration.'

Cherry Picking
Julia Serano

The first time I learned about sex was in 5th grade. It wasn't by way of a sex education class or a Mom and Dad birds-and-the-bees speech, but rather a joke. A completely unfunny dirty joke little kids tell to pass along important information. I think the punch line was, "Mommy, Mommy, turn on your headlights! Daddy's snake is about to go into your cave!" Now, granted before hearing the joke I already had a strange relationship with my penis. I used to draw pictures of myself naked with a needle going into my penis, imagining that it contained special medicine that would make the thing disappear. Every time I used the urinal in the little boy's room, I had a sneaking suspicion something wasn't quite right. That night, after hearing the joke, I remember looking down at my penis, knowing what it was supposedly for, and I felt absolutely detached and dumbfounded.

The first time I dressed as a girl was in 6th grade. I had insomnia and one night I felt compelled to wrap a pair of white lacy curtains around my body. I stared at my reflection in the bedroom mirror for hours. I looked like a girl. Perhaps it should have been no surprise. I was pre-pubescent and had one of those longish, late '70s, boy haircuts. But it completely blew my mind. The scariest part about this revelation was that it somehow made perfect sense.

The first time I had a crush on someone was in 7th grade. Her name was Kathy and I thought she was cute. Nancy Phillips told me that Kathy liked me but I was too chicken-shit to ask her out. So I fantasized about her instead. I imagined some bad guy had captured us both and as part of his evil scheme he would offer me two choices: he would either kill Kathy or turn me into a girl. He left it up to me to decide and I would always gallantly choose the latter. Kathy would be so impressed that I had sacrificed my maleness to save her life that she would ask me out on a date. I always said yes, and the rest of the fantasy involved different permutations of the two of us sucking face. All of this happened before I ever heard the word "lesbian."

The first time I decided to change my sex was in 10th grade. It happened at my baseball league all-star game. I wasn't playing in the game but I went with a few friends who also didn't make the team. While we were sitting in the bleachers, a group of neighborhood girls walked by and some of my flirtier guy friends started teasing them in that teenage-boy "I like you" sort of way. Both groups struck up a conversation but I just sort of sat there and stared. It seemed so obvious to me that I should be one of those girls rather than one of these boys. It was so sad because nobody could see it but me. So I decided to get a sex change operation. I didn't really know what it was or what it involved, I had only heard about it on TV. Later I realized if I was to pursue such a thing I would have to let all of my friends and family know I wanted to be a girl, and I couldn't think of anything more frightening. So, instead, I tucked the memory of my all-star game epiphany into the dark recesses of my brain. Like a time capsule, I wouldn't come across it again for another fifteen years.

The first time I had a girlfriend was in 12th grade. She was smart and quirky and interesting and cute and completely kick-ass. I totally fell for her; she was my first true love. After dates, we would park on a quiet, dark street and make out. Her lips were the first ones I ever kissed, her breasts the first I felt up, her vagina the first I fingered. She was one year younger than me but way more mature. When I left to go to college, she suggested we see other people. I was devastated but she said that we were both still really young and had our whole lives ahead of us. She was right.

My first supposed sexual peak came when I was eighteen. It was my first year of college and I didn't really have any freshman sexual experiences to speak of. Some years are just like that but don't feel bad for me, I made up for it by having a second sexual peak as a woman at the age of thirty-five.

The first time that I masturbated to orgasm was when I was nineteen. Nobody ever believes that it happened so late but it's true. Before then, when I'd play with myself, I would push down on my penis and rock my hand back and forth. I've since been told that that's how a lot of girls do it. I just did it that way instinctually. It felt really good but I never orgasmed. Then my college girlfriend gave me my first hand job and I learned the power of the stroke. Granted, I knew about the stroke from watching porn but it never occurred to me to try it out on myself. It worked like a charm. It's amazing how you can have a body all of your life yet there's always something new that you can learn about it. Strangely enough, I don't really remember the first time that I had penetrative sex, the supposedly landmark day when my virginity was officially lost. It's true. I know it happened when I was nineteen with the girlfriend I had throughout most of college. I've lost the particular night we popped each other's cherries in a blur of dorm room sex scenes the two of us shared over a three-year period. Eventually she went on the pill, and since we were each other's first, we stopped using condoms. I could never get over how amazing it felt to be inside her, to feel my genitals inside her genitals. To this day, that feeling is the only part about being physically male that I fondly reminisce about.

The first time that I ever went out in public dressed as a woman was when I was twenty-one. I came home from college for Easter weekend while the rest of my family was away on a trip. I shaved off the silly-looking beard I had grown over the semester. I put on my sister's black cotton knit dress. It had long sleeves so no one could see my arm hair and I wore opaque tights to hide my leg hair. I'm sure I put way too much make-up on my face and way too much product in my hair but nobody seemed to care because it was the '80s. I drove to a mall about an hour away from my parent's house so I wouldn't run into anyone who knew me. As I approached the entrance, an older man held the door open for me and called me "sweetie." I felt flattered and insulted at the same time but mostly I was just amazed to be getting away with it. After walking around the mall for about ten minutes, I realized I was hungry and hadn't eaten all morning. I drove to a Burger King for a shake and fries. The woman at the drive-thru window said, "Thank you, ma'am," as she handed me my change and receipt. I can't begin to tell you how beautiful those three simple words sounded.

The first time I told someone that I cross-dressed was when I was twenty-three. He was a friend of a friend and we were hanging out at a party. Out of the blue, he told me he was bisexual and he thought I was cute. I told him that I wasn't into boys but I did like dressing up as a girl. We talked about it all for a couple of hours. When I woke up the following morning, I practically died of embarrassment.

The first time I kissed a boy was when I was twenty-four. It happened in the Bronx. I was coming to terms with my submissive fantasies and met a dominant guy through a personal ad he had placed in the *Village Voice*. In my fantasies I was always female but I was afraid to go to his place cross-dressed, so instead I went in drab (tranny talk for "dressed as a boy"). When I got there, he was dressed head-to-toe in leather and reeked of patchouli. His stereo was blasting Depeche Mode, which seemed really cliché. He tied me up to his bed, blindfolded me, and began kissing and groping me. It was extra-weird because he had a moustache and I kept imagining that his mouth was some strange combination of a porcupine and a leech. It wasn't a lot of fun. I'm sure he didn't enjoy himself much either, what with me being a confused and inexperienced bottom who just sort of lay there doing nothing. Afterwards, we both talked about our favorite Woody Allen films. I never saw him again.

The first time I had sex with someone while in femme mode was when I was twenty-eight. She was a bisexual friend who I dated on and off for a bit. First we went to the SF MoMA to see a Frida Kahlo exhibit. Then we went back to her place and shared a bottle of wine. We kissed. She fondled my foam breast through my shirt and told me how much she missed being with a woman. She lent me some clothes that were less dorky than the ones I had on, and she took it upon herself to re-do my make-up and hair. She made me look way better than I did earlier that day. We left her house to go to the Chameleon, a local dive bar. She laughed when the Latino boys in her neighborhood made the snake sounds at me. We had a few beers and talked. It was like two girls talking, she even said so. We both cried at one point. I'm not exactly sure why but in retrospect I think it was because we both realized how sad it was that I had to keep this part of me hidden most of the time. Afterwards we went back to her place and had sloppy sex. She wanted me to penetrate her but I couldn't keep it up. How could I after all of that? The next morning, I woke up and realized I didn't bring any boy clothes along because I wasn't planning on spending the night. She lent me a pair of her pants and a hockey jersey to wear on the return trip to my apartment. She was a lot bigger than me so when I put on the shirt it felt like I was wearing a tent. I seemed so small. I can't remember ever feeling less like a boy than I did sitting on the BART train wearing that hockey jersey.

I met Dani, who would eventually become my wife, when I was

thirty. We shared lots of firsts together. She was the first dyke activist that I ever dated, the first person I ever moved in with, the first person I shared a checking account with. We even merged our CD collections. She was the first person to take me with a strap-on dildo, the first to give me a purely anal orgasm, the first person who truly understood how to make love to my physically male body while relating to me as a woman. Dani was by my side the day I first called myself "queer" and the day I first dared to refer to myself as "transgendered." She was the first and only person I ever asked to marry me. On a rainy night, during the brief period when we were calling each other "fiancée," the two of us were lying in our bed. I told her I was thinking about transitioning. We held hands and talked about it through the night. In the morning she took me out to breakfast by Lake Merritt. She made me laugh. Somehow she made the scariest day of my life really, really beautiful.

The first time I took female hormones was when I was thirty-three. It was the day after our honeymoon. I washed the pills down with water, then sat on the balcony of our apartment waiting for the buzz to hit.

The first time I had a female orgasm was about two months after that. I was masturbating, and for the first time in my life the stroke just wasn't doing it. I just needed... more. So I grabbed Dani's Hitachi Magic Wand. A few years back I had tried out her vibrators but they were way too much stimulation for my male organ. But now, after two months of being on female hormones, I could place her vibrator directly onto the tip of my penis and... Wow! Suddenly I found myself writhing for ten or fifteen minutes straight, in a sexual state at least twenty times more intense than any boy orgasm I had ever had. I decided right there and then I was never going back.

The first day I lived as a woman was a day that Dani and I planned to celebrate. On our honeymoon, she bought an expensive bottle of wine for us to share on that special occasion. However, some firsts don't happen in a very clear-cut fashion. There was no first day of being female for me. Instead, I just gradually changed over a five-month period and before I knew it, strangers were referring to me as "she" even though I was still dressing in drab. We ended up drinking that bottle of wine on our wedding anniversary instead.

Some people have asked if I will become a virgin again when I eventually have bottom surgery. You know, a vaginal virgin of sorts. I just laugh. The whole idea of virginity is utterly ridiculous, as if every person's life can be divided up neatly into an innocent child-like half and the impure adult half. People who believe this must have excruciatingly boring and simplistic sex lives.

For me, there have been many first times and each has given me a rare opportunity to see myself a bit differently. My life has no singular defining point because each first time is dependent upon all of the other ones which came previously. And while having surgery may mark the end of my physical transition to female, I don't see my sexual evolution as reaching some sort of conclusion. If there is one thing I've learned, it's that there will always be more first times to look forward to in my future.

Fifty Reasons I Love My Man
Bryn Kelly

I love his big ol' gentle brown eyes. Right this minute, he is also letting me use his laptop to write embarrassing stories about him that may eventually be published. Right this minute, we're in a coffee shop where he has bought me an everything bagel with a schmear, a bottle of cranberry juice with a cup of ice, and my favorite kind of chocolate cookie for dessert. I didn't even have to give him my order because that's what I get every time and he knows it.

Back at home, he lets me feed him just about anything except meat. We both believe that the biggest problem with vegetarian cuisine, as it is widely understood, is that is so often bland and boring. He loves spicy food and I love to cook it for him. The spices I feed him seep out of his pores. He always smells a little like garlic, turmeric, hot chilies, and cinnamon. I love the way he smells, even when he's a little funky.

I love his disdain for meat and I love how it makes me feel morally inferior to him. I will chow down on some beef but my man eats tofu instead. A while ago I convinced him to eat one chicken nugget. I kissed him afterward and he tasted all wrong. His mouth always tastes fresh and wholesome because he never eats animals. Regardless of whether or not I've performed a feat of magic in the kitchen, I can count on him to devour it with gusto. If he goes back for seconds and thirds, I know I got it right.

I love his collection of t-shirts with ratty screen-printed logos for bands, after-school programs, and sports teams he's never played on, and how they all smell like him. I love how I can borrow his 1" buttons and pretend I have a much wider breadth of musical knowledge than I actually do.

I love his weird-ass, socialist summer camp, Westchester family. I love his stories about growing up in a disastrous urban intentional community that combined the worst elements of Maoist Marxism, radical psychotherapy, and musical theater. I love imagining him in plays where all the kids boo the kid wearing the Ronald Reagan mask. I love how his mom once told me about a year when he protested Thanksgiving dinner out of solidarity with the turkey.

He tells me funny stories about his brothers and sisters, like when his little sister was eight and ran up to a bunch of other kids, pulled down her pants, and started to yell, "I have a butt! I have a butt! Look at my butt!" Now she's a big-shot public policy wonk at Harvard, and she makes me feel like some kind of bucolic hayseed who fell off the manure truck and landed in Cobble Hill.

"Oh, it's crazy running into you two like this! Where are you off to? The Magnolia Bakery?" She flips her wrist toward me. "Oh, this must be your doing. I mean, it's a little, you know, *Sex and the City*." Isn't that a cunty thing to say? Like I'm some kind of Metro North bitch who decided to come into the City for some cupcakes as a fun alternative to the White Plains Galleria. But then I picture her mooning a bunch of little boys on the playground and feel better.

I love how he can handle going down-home with me into the deep hollers of West Virginia. I love how he can deal with going to my mama's stadium-sized, charismatic Pentecostal mega-church, and how he gets a kick out of it when it's time for some faith healin'. I love how he keeps his sense of humor when my brother-in-law grills him about vegetarianism. "You mean, you don't eat beef? You don't eat chicken? You don't eat bacon? Ham? Steak? Deer? Squirrel?"

I love how we both realized at such a young age that idealism is a rough road and that utopias are almost always bound to fail. I love how we keep giving it a shot anyway.

I love the way he is completely enraptured by art. I love the way he sits, enthralled, way back on those leather benches at the Wexner Center for Contemporary Art, swinging his feet like a little boy. I love how he drags my ass all over Chelsea and uptown and downtown and out to Queens all in one day, all for the sake of absorbing as much art as possible. I love holding his hand while we wander through the trippy circus-mirror corridors of a Yayoi Kusama installation, and how he squeezes my hand when he points out Felix Gonzalez Torres' twin clocks, Perfect Lovers.

Once we fucked hard and rough all night, and went to the art museum the next day where we saw paintings filled with mucosal red splotches and I was like, "Ugh. That looks like what just came out of my butt in the bathroom fifteen minutes ago." Sometimes I recall this moment and it makes me happy.

I love that he only owns two pairs of shoes, one of which is a pair of snow boots. He always remembers where my keys are when I lose them, and always knows where his phone is so he can call mine when I lose it.

He wakes me up every morning with my get-going cocktail: a cup of green tea, my vitamins, and my estrogen. I like to sleep late and it takes at least an hour to make myself beautiful or at least feel okay about going outside. He's okay with the fact that our bedroom is a flurry of make-up brushes, hair extensions, styling appliances and product. We have this very Miss-Piggy-and-Kermit thing going on.

Sometimes he lets me do him up with make-up and wigs. Amazingly, my attempts at force-feminization only make him look more virile, like some kind of glam barbarian warrior fighting cyber-imperial rule.

Fiction and media portrayals of trans people in relationships (particularly romantic or sexual) tend to take on the characteristics of a morality play, and tend toward exhibiting a fairly short range of dynamics: from violent to pathetic to exploitative to prematurely aborted, usually due to some kind of crazy thing involving disclosure. I can honestly say that of all the representations of trans relationships I've seen, very few mention happy relationships, supportive partners, or love that exists outside of "deception" or accelerated tragedy, and that goes doubly for representations of trans women who love men. A sort of cultural folk wisdom exists in some trans women's communities that the only way to be truly loved and appreciated by your partner, especially if your partner is a man, is to make 100% sure that your pre-transition past never becomes part of the story of your relationship. This obviously creates a sort of double-bind wherein trans women are encouraged to keep our pasts a secret to protect our relationships yet admonished for being deceitful when we decide not to disclose.

I love how I can drag his ass to trans-related stuff and he is totally nonplussed. I love how he can be the only non-trans person in a room and not think there's anything all that unusual. By that same token, his main anxiety around being involved with a trans woman is a fear that people in progressive queer communities are going to think he's with me out of a misguided attempt at queer cred. He's worried about being seen as a gay poseur. Aww.

I know that some people who know about my trans history might have a few questions about his sexuality but one thing I love about him is how he really has no problems with it. When I ask him, "Are you ever worried that people might think you're gay?" He says, "Nah. Besides, there's nothing wrong with being gay." That's really the end of it for him: there's nothing wrong with being gay.

Now I'm not trying to hate but I'm really glad he doesn't identify as an "admirer" or a trannychaser or a SOFFA (Significant Other, Friend, Family, and Ally). It's kind of a relief that he considers himself a standard-issue straight guy. Don't get me wrong: I certainly wouldn't mind if he were queer. In fact, I have attempted as best I can to turn him into fag-bait. I'll ask him, "Check out that guy. Would you fuck that guy? How about him? What kind of guy would you fuck if you had to fuck a guy?" but he'll have none of it. He just loves the ladies, no matter what I do.

He tells me I'm smart all of the time except when it's sexy to tell me I'm a stupid slut. He's always buying me presents, trinkets, baubles, and toys, because he's my Daddy and he loves me.

His ass can't drive but it looks cute on a bicycle.

I love how he never fails to tell me I look pretty even when I'm the messiest of messes. Even when I suspect he may be stretching the truth a little, he still manages to sound sincere. When my hair looks crazy and sticks out like a rag doll, when all my make-up is smeared off my face (especially after giving him a particularly long and sloppy blowjob), when I'm all puffy and bleary-eyed, when my ass is dripping from having been fucked so hard, or even when I've been crying all day long. I am a person with a shit ton of appearance issues and he manages to soothe them out so expertly, like he's applying a balm to my raw, exposed skin.

He tells me secrets he won't tell anyone else.

I will never forget how he held me when the nurse at the health department told me I was HIV-positive and how he held me while I sobbed and mourned for days which eventually turned into weeks and months. There are a million reasons he could have dropped me like a rock and no one, not even I, would have faulted him. The guilt I felt was compounded by the fact that we had been having unprotected sex almost daily, sometimes multiple times a day, for almost nine months before we both got tested. I found out I was positive and he remains negative to this day. This probably has a lot to do with the ways we have sex but we're still really lucky.

He braces me while I wait on labs and is the scaffolding around me while I wait to hear the news. If my CD4 count has fallen or if my viral load has risen, if these numbers mean it's time to start on meds, if I'm going to start losing weight and lose the tits and ass I've worked so hard to get, or if I'm going to start getting the explosive poops and other assorted bugs, he is there. These days, I live by numbers, and he helps me translate these numbers into words, words like "hope" and "courage" and "today."

The first time we hooked up, I wondered if we had discovered some kind of sexual utopia. Our bed became our own little pleasure city on a hill where we explored all the nooks and crannies of our desires, where we fought, giggled, and whispered. It was all contrasts and textures: my smooth milky skin against his fuzzy olive skin, my fingers through his woolly black hair ,and his strong hands grabbing a fistful of my long, silky, fiery red hair. I was so surprised to find someone to whom I was so deeply attracted, who was into all the stuff I liked, and who wasn't hung up on the trans thing. The H-bomb certainly upset all that for a while.

We have since learned that for many serodiscordant couples it is most often the positive partner who is more reluctant to resume sexual activity out of feeling guilty, dirty, and unlovable. There is often a misguided attempt to "protect" the other partner from him or herself. I definitely had those feelings but I also wanted sexual comfort. We both had the specter of this disease hanging out over our bed while we fumbled and figured out how to make this very unsexy situation sexy once again.

After a lot of communication, we got back to doing the nasty. He will wear a condom to fuck me even though he hates wearing condoms. He hates wearing condoms because his dick is so big. Did I mention that already? Now don't get me wrong, I know how stretchy and pliable they are, but trust me, I've been around and some guys just need a little extra room. So we buy the Lifestyles Kings and get down to business. It kind of embarrasses him when I rhapsodize about his dick but I think he likes it.

We had a long talk about the possibility of getting married a little while ago. Clearly, marriage is a big step and one that is dubiously legal in our case since in many regards my legal gender changes depending on which country, state, county, and municipality I happen to find myself in. Still, we've considered it. I've expressed a lot of concern that getting married will lead to some kind of desensitized, white-flight, suburban, Pottery Barn existence based on American capitalist imperial values. His response? "You know, if there's one thing I want in a wife, it's a wife who hates America."

He subscribes to the *New Yorker*, *Harper's*, *the Nation*, and *Mother Jones*. One time he took a series of dirty pictures of me fucking myself with a cute purple dildo while reading Karl Marx, Michel Foucault, Noam Chomsky, Naomi Klein, and Saul Alinsky.

We are both messy people and we're messy together. He's the best roommate I've ever had. Before him, I always lived with other girls—specifically the kind of girls who, though we saw each other six times a day, would tend to leave annoying passive-aggressive notes on the fridge saying things like, "Could the person who drank my almond milk please replace it? It is a very important ingredient in my agave-gingko-buckwheat smoothie at 6 a.m. every day as I am currently on a 700-calorie-a-day diet which is dangerous if not done consistently and accurately." With him, it's like, "Oh, man, there's no more almond milk. Let's go get some more almond milk."

When I'm feeling sick, I can stay home and look at weird things all day on the internet, like serial killers who have blogs, and when he gets home from work I can tell him all the details I learned about serial killers with blogs, and not only does he listen but he's interested and asks questions. "Really, he was from Akron?" and "No, I did not know that Rammstein was still around!"

Right this minute, I love how he's looking at me, wondering what I'm writing about him, how I can pretty much predict his reaction to every passage, and how he will probably nit-pick every detail: "My sister is in graduate school; she is not a wonk."

Right this minute, I love how nervous he is that I'm going to spill something on his beloved iBook G4, my one true rival for his affection. I love that our relationship is complicated and weird and textured - not quite perfect, not quite ideal, not quite a utopia. I love how he has crumbs on his chin, and how he probably has latté breath by now. I love his natty hoodie and busted Chucks. I love his three-day scruff.

I love the way we work it out.

Believing Is Seeing
Silas Howard

Every moment is two moments, parallel lines like train tracks that appear to join at the horizon. There are two stories, the one told and the one happening. When you sneeze your heart stops, comically. We hold together a universe of perfectly timed mistakes and near misses. Making up our own fables and cautionary tales is a decision. What it demands is faith. What it opens is possibility.

My producer, Effie, a black woman with fire-engine red hair, and I, a white, tattooed, trans guy, drive through a quaint neighborhood in Spokane, Washington, a town once known for its neo-Nazi activities. Our goal is to meet Kitty Tipton, a hard-bitten white Southern woman who did burlesque in the 1950s.

We have nightmares before meeting Kitty, anxious to have her like us and about the fact that we want her permission to make a film about her husband. Kitty was Billy Tipton's last wife, and I co-wrote a screenplay inspired by his story. Billy Tipton, a jazz musician in the 1940s and '50s, was discovered at his death to have been born female. The music world and his family, which included three sons and four ex-wives, claimed no knowledge of this prior to the coroner's discovery in 1989.

On an otherwise serene block, one house stands out from the rest. Instead of a manicured lawn, the yard is filled with plastic bottles and broken toys woven into the overgrown vines. Old, rusted signs are stuffed in hedges and in the ground are stakes with attached plastic bags that billow and rustle in the wind like quixotic sails. In the window is a huge, sun-faded poster of a cat clinging to a tree branch with 'Hang In There Till Friday!' printed underneath. This house reminds me of the apartment of my grandmother, who went crazy after witnessing her mother institutionalized. Insanity didn't just run in my family, it galloped.

Once inside, our eyes adjusted to the dark room where an old woman on the edge of dementia sat in a recliner next to a bed piled three feet high with stuffed animals. A nurse with sad big hair and surprised eyebrows helped Kitty up, placing a pillow behind her back.

"Sit," Kitty commands. She looks us up and down, then points to a velvet painting on the wall directly behind her. It's a painting of a young woman lying naked by a pond, her body outstretched as her hand dips into the water. Behind her is a volcano mid-eruption. "That's me," she says. "The artist was in love with me." She gazed at her young body in the velvety grass for a beat, then back at us. "And that volcano?" Her eyes sparkled. "That's me, too."

We watch tape after tape of interviews Kitty did after Billy died. News crews from Europe, Japan, and the US descended upon this small, broken family. In every interview Kitty refuses to call Billy anything but "he" and maintains that her marriage wasn't a lie; that he was the best husband she could have asked for. In the storm of unremitting questions, her story remained unchanged, repeating like a song. No matter how ignoble the show or incendiary the interviewer, she never, ever sold Billy out.

"You know it wasn't just me, the whole world saw him as male. He shaved, he played in clubs... we played in clubs together. I was an entertainer, too, you know. A dancer. I worked in clubs owned by the Mafia. One time I didn't like how this man grabbed me and I went backstage, got my gun, came out, and shot at him."

She reaches for my hand but forgets mid-way. "If you go home and take your girlfriend's hand and hold it up to your man hand, you'll see the difference. Billy had male hands." I picture Billy at the piano; he used to wait till the whole band was on stage to excuse himself to go the men's room, knowing that was the safest time.

"I won't talk to you about the sex. Everyone wants to know about that, not going to tell you about how we had sex," she says. I tell her we're interested in Billy as a musician and their love story. I'm searching for the details of the daily improv of a jazzman, creating on the edge of nothing. Music has the power to make one lose their sex, their limits, their memory. Like love or a leap of faith. To not know what will happen but do it anyway. I don't say all this but that's the real story I'm after.

"You're lucky I like you. I like your voice," she goes on, "usually I tell people to get the fuck out of here." She holds up her middle finger up to an imaginary visitor. As we get ready to leave, Kitty asks Effie to take a photo of her and me. SNAP. Just as the camera clicks, Kitty hikes up her nightgown above the knee, showing off her gams, a grin across her face.

You walk in the bar, late for our first meeting. Your arms reach out and hug the person next to me. SNAP. Without missing a beat, you pose for the camera, still hugging the person, then look at me and smile. The club promoter takes your picture again; the moment officially captured. You make a good entrance, I think as I smile at you.

A few months prior you emailed me in response to my search for a lead to play Billy Tipton, which eventually led to this first meeting. We talked of the project, of people who might audition, of wanting to do things that matter. My friend said I should meet you, said you had this quality about you, that you spoke your mind no matter what the cost. I felt that spark of recognition right away. Your old school glamour, mordant wit, and those beautifully fucked-up teeth: an intoxicating combination. A fellow escape artist. I remember you made fun of me for saying I was a Gemini, so West Coast. And then you caught me looking at you. It was not a look intended to seduce you; it was a look that showed what I probably meant to keep hidden. Something is happening. "Come to Los Angeles," I say. "Come to San Francisco," you say. And I did.

Fence sneaking and trespassing, we hide from the cop... badly, and are caught, but after-thankfully-our visit to those huge letters staggered across the hill. H for Hollywood. H for you. The letters look so straight from below but up close they are a crooked little line of simple corrugated metal cut-outs spelling out a real estate marketing ploy. Hollywood Land. We hold tight, down in the dirt, skirt up around your thighs. I can see us from above, we're so small, those letters seared on our brains from childhood. Escape. Dream factory. We're secrets, down there in the corner of the letter H, three stories tall. We are massive, among all those stars.

Before meeting Kitty, Effie and I had dinner with one of Billy's three sons. He sold the movie rights over a decade ago to some Hollywood producer and the sale caused friction in his family. Each member claimed a portion of their father's life and one son even broke into his booking agency to steal files to sell off. The thievery could have staved off grief, but not forever. This son had a similar glint of mischief in his eyes as his mother. Though Kitty adopted all three boys I could see influences of her in his mannerism.

"I was much more excited to meet you after I saw your picture online," he says through a roguish smile at Effie. She's good at fending off his advances with humor, saving us from an awkward meal together. He told us that Billy was a good dad, taught him right from wrong, about women and fixing cars. He paid the news reporter $1,000 to hold the coroner's report until after Billy's funeral, to let him be the man they always knew him to be for one day longer.

We head to a local sports bar and meet his friends. I haven't transitioned yet and get introduced as "she." The woman across the table looks me dead in the eye and asks casually if I ever felt like a man trapped in a woman's body.

I say, "Well, kind of I do."

She points to the biggest, burliest man in the bar and says, "So when you're looking at a woman, it's like you're looking through his eyes?"

I shrug my shoulders. "I guess it's... something like that." I am perplexed but also amazed at her personal deconstruction of gender. She then returns to talk about real estate while John flirts with Effie, telling her stories about sea diving, adoption, and how he can't wait to be on set when we make the movie about his dad.

Billy brought us together again when you asked to see the scenes I directed for a director's lab. I cast a trans/butch guy for the role of Billy, and got to see the movie come to life, if only for a scene or two. We went back at midnight to where I was staying under the pretense of watching the scenes.

Hours go by, or does time fool us? From the window, a magnificent skyline and gleaming façades. We blend into the shadows, my shirt drenched in sweat, at the waterfront, the bridges, the nape of your neck and other ordinary miracles. Enjoying the imprudent hues of scheming dreams. Too early for dawn, but not night either. Blue pools of light, a city of historical mysteries, a place we can invent for ourselves.

"It's about duplicity, deception, and their sex life," says the man.

"No, actually it's not," I start to say. Every point I counter, he picks a new one. This studio executive is legendary. People say how darn smart he is yet he doesn't seem to get it. I recently received an email from a 70-year-old man Billy used to play music with, who thanked me for calling Billy "he." This guy probably knew two gay people his whole life, living in a small town, and yet he understands that Billy is a man. Meanwhile Mr. Hollywood can't get it, even though he's probably gay.

Perhaps they want more drama (subtext: how the outsider fools the straights and lives a life of 'lies' as a result), full of dirty details to baffle and intrigue. I can't imagine serving up a movie that reduces Billy's whole life to the fact that a coroner discovered his body didn't match his gender. It's not a question of gender, really, but of one's life in relation to their actions and contributions to the world. Couldn't we instead take the most tabloid topic possible and produce something more surprising and subtle: a musing on the nature of love?

He scans the air for obstacles; it's a cat and mouse game. At times I'm the mouse... well, mostly I'm the mouse. But for a moment I'm the cat ready to strike, to kill my chance rather then see it slowly dismembered and toyed with. Almost all films could be titled *Trapped*, someone once said.

The next day my development executive calls to say she's proud of me for standing by the project. The studio executive we met with told her how incredibly "well-adjusted" he thought I was.

"What the hell does that mean?" Effie says into the phone.

Who knew that all I had to do to become well-adjusted was move to Hollywood?

We get our film back from the studio, which they are good enough to provide in spite of the money they invested in developing the film, though it was mainly because of Effie who produced numerous award-winning films with them. Within four months we have another offer. Full financing from a payroll company. The company consists of two guys, John and Ron, who do the payroll for half of the film industry.

John's tattooed forearm waves in the air as he speaks. "You, you're a director, you make movies. Me, I'm god, I make people." He chuckles looking around the table.

"That's hot," Effie says. She finds him appalling and appealing at the same time, a perfect film industry symbol.

The money and contract come fast and they look good. I try to ignore my gut which tells me that this guy just wants to hit on actresses and perhaps even wants to direct the film himself. He asks if I want to read one of his scripts. Everyone says, "Just take it... it's real money, take it... no one offers full financing like this," but I don't trust the guy. Then they start acting crazy, arguing and bullying us over contract points, using big words I have to look up like "anathema"... and all through texting! We walk. Two months later the company goes belly-up overnight. Turns out they had swimsuit models on payroll, fancy Hollywood hills parties, and money laundering. Effie sends me an email reading only, "We dodged a bullet." I just want to tell the story of a guy and his search to find home.

You make me think of home, or rather like home should be. A friend once pointed out that for people like us, home was something to escape from, not recreate. But the gaze is seductive; the act of seeing and being seen place us, connects us to one another. I struggle with naming things: it's tedious and consuming, it gives and it takes, changes and at times embarrasses. But on wild nights who can call you home? Only those who know you by name.

I invite you to walk with me; the night air turns cool and gun metal blue. I offer my coat and the moment of possibility as your hand reaches for my leg on the Ferris wheel. From a great height, above the glittering city, our feet dangle over the boardwalk.

There's a parade happening all the time, we decide, you just need to pay attention. This particular one is started by a lone Goth girl singing Danzig followed by her two friends shout-talking about an 8-ball. Behind them a tugboat goes slow and steady, lights festive in the dark water. You pull off your high heels as we climb a pile of rubble that is destined to become new condos along the water. Soon we won't be able to afford to sit here but for now it is ours for the taking. We look at the stars blinking, planets not blinking. Reveries of travel, not so much to run from memories but to find the perfect one.

When I was a kid I believed if I looked hard enough across the Atlantic Ocean I could see France. I was certain of the logic that desire equaled attainment. I'd draw plans for a time travel machine to explore supernatural worlds that takes the simplest of facts, like the rotation of the earth, and make a personal religion out of it. I believed there must always be exceptions to a rule. It gave me the feeling that I could control things with my mind.

Kitty died this past May, 2008. I had planned to visit her this summer, to get her stories recorded before they were lost. The last thing she said to me was to make sure to come back soon and not to forget her. I try and keep people alive by remembering them with a fastidious tenderness. Love can only be as good as the lover.

I picture Billy in his halcyon days casting long, hard looks at Kitty in the bar where they did shows together; the jazzman and the burlesque dancer. They say sound travels forever if there is no friction to slow it down, but a world without friction is one with no movement, remaining in the same state forever, there would be no light or smell or feel.

> *You've got to give a little, take a little,*
> *And let your poor heart break a little.*
> *That's the story of, that's the glory of love.*

A jazz player lives at the edge of disaster. It's neither sweet nor harmonious; it's nonsense and chaos, madness and dreams.

Excerpt from the play
B4T (before testosterone)
Imani Henry

Keith Rodman is 30 years old and African-American. It's after work and Keith is dressed in a beige suit, white shirt, and orange and blue striped tie. He is being interviewed and videotaped by Ashanti, an African-American woman, for her graduate school thesis. Moments ago, Keith and Ashanti were in an argument.

Keith slowly walks back to his chair and sits.

You want to hear something funny? I had never been with no lesbian before. I met Geneva at a college party my boy took me to. Back before I was on hormones, I wasn't the type to just step to a woman. I wasn't brave like that. It would be like, I'd look and she'd look. And if she smiled, then I knew it was cool to step to her.

Now, mind you, most times they didn't know they were looking at another female. Sometimes they knew but they just don't want to admit it, which was cool with me. Then there were them times that they knew exactly who they looking at and for that reason they start smiling at you. But I never been with no woman that called herself a lesbian. So I'm at this party, out on the porch drinking a 40, talking to this dude that I knew from one of my classes. And Geneva came up and said, "Hi."

Not one of those regular "Hi"s. She was, like, **(does gesture and in a high pitch voice)** "Hi!" You know, all sexy and shit. I was thinking, "Well, that's some brave shit," cuz she did it right in front of that dude.

So she started talking to both of us, but you know, really just to me. I guess he got the hint, cuz finally he just walked away. Geneva was FINE. I mean, not that permed hair, all made-up kinda fine that I was used to. Geneva was natural. Back then she had one of them high-top fades and wore little lipstick. To tell the truth, I really didn't even know what was happening. I mean, back then, when I was with a woman, I would do most of the talking. But Geneva, she was asking me questions about myself. Telling me things about herself. I just thought, maybe this is just how college girls are.

So we're talking and it's going mad good. Then she asked me how long I'd been out. And I was like, **(looks at watch)** "Since about 9 o'clock."

She laughed! Then she was like, **(in Geneva voice)** "Oh, no, I mean, how long have you been out as a lesbian?"

I was like, "A what?" And I guess the look on my face must've scared her cuz she was, like, "Ooh, no, I didn't mean to offend you."

To tell you the truth, I had just never had no woman ask me that before. It kinda threw me. But I recovered. So I was, like, **(re-enacts, very sincere)** "Well, if the question is, 'Do I like women?' Then the answer is, 'Yes.' "

She like that. Then I was, like, **(more suave)** "If the question is, 'Do I like you?'... Then the answer is, 'Definitely yes.' " She really like that one.

So anyway, Geneva and me, we keep talking, and it was starting to be about that time. You know, *that time* **(looks around)**. But I wasn't gonna do nothing in front of them people at the party. I guess Geneva musta been scheming too, cuz she was, like, "Do you want to come back to my room?"

So I was like, "Peace!" to my boy that I came with, and me and Geneva, we go back to her room and I get there and I looking around. I was, like, "Damn, this girl sure like purple." She had a purple rug, purple sheets, purple bedspread. She had pictures on the wall of women kissing. Then I look and I see this sign that says, "Lesbian Rights Now!" And I'm thinking to myself, "But she's Black." Up until that time I didn't know nobody who call themselves gay 'cept white people.

So anyway, me and Geneva, **(pauses)** we start kissing, and it's going real good! She ain't pulling away, flippin' out or nothing. I mean, back then I knew it would take women time to get used to me touching them. Then they would get over it and then... you don't need to know this. Anyway, everything was going real cool... **(pauses to remember)** Oh, yeah! Everything was going real cool until she started reaching for my chest. Now, again, back then if a woman started reaching, I'd be like **(does slow 'hands off' gesture)** and she'd be so nervous she wouldn't do that no more.

But Geneva wasn't having it! It fact, she was kind of wild! Her hands were going **(touches all the 'vital' body parts with lines and then stands)** here, and here, and here and then here... and soon I just had to get up. I ain't even been felt up by no dude. I didn't want to be felt up by a woman.

(Sits back down) So then Geneva, she sits up on the bed, and she like, "You're a stone butch, huh?" I didn't even know what that was but it sounded good. Then she got up off the bed, walking towards me, all sexy and shit, hips just going to the side, Pow! Pow! Then she sits on my lap. She puts her arms around my neck and says, "How a big ol' strong boy like you gonna be afraid of little ol' me?" Then she started kissing my neck, and on my face.

(Comes out of reenactment) I ain't gonna go into all the details because, you know, I'm a gentleman. But let me tell you... Lesbians are the shit! Ten years! Geneva and me. That's my wife. That's my heart.

Sleeping Fruity
Timea Quon

I've always wanted fairy tale happiness and romance. As a kid, I pored over books of fairy tales, drifting into the stories, and daydreaming of the day I would be rescued by a prince on a horse. I would be awakened from eternal slumber by his kiss, fitted with the glass slipper, and taken as his bride. It was a trifle alarming when, during the onset of puberty, things went a tad awry. As I progressed into my teens, I was shocked that my hair did not grow out long and lustrous and my voice did not turn into the lilting singsong of a canary. Instead, my voice went deep and baritone, and my hair was unruly.

Where were the birds to sit with on my porch and serenade me with the neighborhood mice? In a frenzy, I went back to my books, scanning furiously for anything that reflected my life as it was slowly developing. Unfortunately, there was no story of any Sleeping Beauty who, when woken by her Prince Charming's kiss must conceal a raging case of morning wood. And, sadly, my size-ten foot would not fit into the dainty glass slipper. I would be doomed to serve my ugly stepsisters well into spinsterhood. Apparently, I had been screwed over by an illusion. No birds would be singing, save for the terrible crow outside my window at ungodly hours of the morning. It seemed that there would be no prince either. At only 13, my dreams had been crushed.

One can imagine my sense of relief at age 16 when I first looked up the definition of the word "transgender." Here was a title most fitting. It was like finding the correct block for the right-shaped hole. With this new definition, I could evidently give a big "fuck you" to teenage boyhood and right past wrongs. And quite possibly, just maybe, I could meet my Prince Charming after all.

Shortly after my discovery I began the process of transitioning from male to female. I grew my hair long, embracing my natural curls. I pumped up my now hormone-induced chest (read: buds, mosquito bites) with padded bras, and bought the skankiest of skirts and fishnet stockings. I made up my face with the finest drugstore make-up worthy of the title "whore paint." Come hell or high water, I would be the Princess. I would snag my Prince Charming. And, for damn sure, I would have my fairy tale romance.

Oddly enough, the men did not come knocking. I look back on that past with a lingering sense of dread and a feeling of good old-fashioned nausea. Really, despite having soft features due to an Asian lineage, I was a mockery of womanhood. I had no guidance, no fairy godmother (or fairy dragmother), to bestow upon me the knowledge of appropriate femininity that would have suited my personality and body. My guidebooks for femininity were the rags off the drugstore magazine rack that promised beauty and above all else, love, to those who followed their preaching. I looked rather pathetic, like someone playing dress-up or make believe, rather than someone merely dressing for the day. It's a wonder I got any attention at all.

There were some men, the trannychasers. They were not so much princes as they were vile trolls under the bridge, offering accolades and compliments galore for the opportunity to get in my pants. They didn't have bucking steeds, and were not interested in long-term romance. All they wanted was a short initial conversation leading to mutual oral and fucking up the ass. They never seemed very interested in meeting the family or discussing the possibility of going away for the weekend. But, sadly, they acted as validation for this newly anointed transexual who could barely stand to look in the mirror. At the time, they made all my plucking, plumping, waxing, and painting worth something. In a society obsessed with the larger-than-life female sex symbol-all big tits and tiny hips-these men were validation that I somehow belonged. Even though it wasn't fairy tale romance, it was closer than what I had before transitioning. This illusory, momentary "love" was better than remaining in the shadows.

During my childhood I couldn't have cared less what other people thought of me. Yes, I wanted fairy tale romance but I would never do anything that felt uncomfortable or compromising to my sense of self. As a teenager I grasped onto feminist politics and sensibilities, admiring those who flouted convention. Yet there I was, parading around like a walking stereotype. Despite the attention of the aforementioned trannychasers, I still berated myself constantly. I would compare myself to biological women and emotionally shit on my small bust, barrel chest, deep voice. I would compare myself to other transwomen who were so much more feminine, and deep down I hated myself.

Then one day it clicked. After two years of awkwardly stumbling through life on too-high heels, I decided I had enough. The clouds did not part, the harps and choirs did not sound in the background, but I was having an epiphany. I can't say what sparked it. Honestly, I don't remember seeing or hearing something. It was as if I was stumbling around in the dark and finally found the light switch. I no longer attempted to pass myself off as any "normal" Betty and Veronica in the world. I no longer compared myself to other transwomen or to biological women, accepting that I did not have the benefit of being born more feminine or female. I accepted that all women are different, trans or not. Most importantly, I no longer settled for the nasty trannychasers who offered momentary thrills and validation but instead searched for something meaningful. I ditched the high heels and skirts for Chucks and jeans. I hacked off my hair and continue to do so gradually every few months. I appreciate my itty-bitty titties and curve-free body, rather than yearn for my bust to resemble that of Jayne Mansfield.

I know what you're thinking. This is the point in the story where I'm supposed to say that I... (a) have had many meaningful and intimate relationships with a variety of genuinely fabulous men, or (b) am married and in love with the man I will die with.

Sadly, I have to burst that bubble, 'cause life ain't no fairy tale now anymore than it was before. Adopting a new sense of self-worth and overall confidence has been beyond beneficial. While it's somewhat improved my interactions with men, it's also brought up a whole host of new and colorful issues. I may exude a sense of confidence in appearance and carriage but tend to clam up when encountering a guy who's cute, funny, smart, or just simply breathing. There's also the inevitable probability that my new, more androgynous femininity causes some confusion. Half the time when I reveal that I'm transexual to strangers, they can't decipher whether I'm male to female or female to male. I don't help the situation when I harbor thoughts of shaving my head or refuse to speak in a higher tone of voice.

Sometimes there are men that gently approach me and stimulate butterflies and rolling waves of nerves in my stomach. And then there are the men who don't recite poetry but rather shout bigoted slurs and wish me death by way of HIV or violent murder. It's a slippery slope to traverse, dating as a transexual. It's even more difficult when a person doesn't actively attempt to fit into the black and white gender binary. I find it quite rare to encounter a heterosexual masculine man that's interested in a transwoman who doesn't have long hair, DD breasts, pouty lips, and a nine-inch penis. With all this negativity, it would seem logical to ditch my newfound confidence for my old self-destructive behaviors. I could quite feasibly start growing my hair out, shortening my hemline, consider breast implants, but all in all I know now that it wouldn't be worth it. Attention from men is not worth the discomfort and deception of my real self. I can only hope that someday I will locate men and women who find a greater variety of body types and genders sexually attractive and worthy of romantic pursuit.

Because I am the gray matter between black and white, the space between male and female, I can only hope that someday there'll be more men who find tomboyish, punky chicks with dicks just as worthy of dating and courtship as the pumped-up bombshell with the perfectly pink pussy at the bar. I can only hope that someday the butches and femmes, the Amazonian women, the sissy boys, and all the gender variants are no longer marginalized as taboo and, even worse, pigeon-holed as fetish material. But until the time when that process of thinking is widespread, I refuse to wait with bated breath for a guy to deem me worthy of his attention. Ultimately, it really should be a matter of whether or not he is worthy of mine.

Jolly Jumper
Shawna Virago

One night I was determined to get off my couch and do something. Anything. I had been a recluse for weeks, just coming home from work at the coffee cart and hiding out in my room ever since I broke up with Stu. True, the relationship had lasted only three days, just as long as the crystal methedrine held out, but it was my record length for a relationship. I also needed to get out because I couldn't ignore the loud squawking coming from the sweater queens I rented my room from, both of whom were screeching unintelligibly at each other over who used the last of the hair products, thus puncturing the fragile balloon of apathy I was trying to cultivate.

I put my hair up in a ponytail and got an outfit together: a mini-skirt, boots, and the baby-doll Stu had shoplifted for me that read Jesus is my Daddy. I grabbed my leather jacket, climbed on my motorcycle, and drove over to Hollywood Billiards on Golden Gate Avenue, between Jones and Market.

I climbed the two flights of red stairs up to the expansive billiards hall which, by the mid-1990s, had seen better days. I looked around and realized I had stumbled into Ladies Night with groups of mostly youngish riot grrl dykes with loud voices shooting pool and ordering beer from sad-faced waitresses. Scanning the room, I quickly deduced I was the only Lady in the joint. Miraculously, I got my own table near the back. I ordered a drink and began working on my pool game.

I had not gone there with the hope of hooking up with anyone. I also thought no one would want to connect with me. Although I had been told I was attractive, I lacked confidence. I had internalized the negative messages from popular culture and the majority of queer culture, both of which agreed that in the hierarchy of life forms being a transexual was considered near the bottom, just above a mitochondrion and right below the nocturnal mollusk. My own dating history had only supported this distorted image. The so-called "straight" men I hooked up with all went on to have committed relationships with other men. Dating dykes had been no better: after dating me they inevitably went out and got boyfriends or husbands, saying they decided they were mostly straight after all. This was all extremely aggravating, especially since I'm a high femme.

I tried other venues for connection such as phone sex but my short attention span made that very unsatisfying. For a while I was in a MTF circle jerk club but that was short-lived. After climaxing none of us could look each other in the eye, wondering if we were perhaps flawed in some way. We would all put our raincoats on in shame and leave the secret clubhouse in silence.

All these complications of my dating life had really caught me off guard. I had envisioned myself ending up as a pampered rich bitch but my sour personality seemed to scare both the sane ones and the rich ones away. A young dyke came up to my table, shaking me from my thoughts.

"Mind if I play?" she asked.

"Yes," I said. As she walked away she gave me the death stare.

I was getting ready to rack up for another game when I noticed someone in my peripheral vision walking in my direction. A tall transwoman in a mechanic's outfit was staring at me, or more accurately staring at my legs.

"Stop looking at my legs," I said, "or buy me a drink."

She kept staring at my legs and ordered me a drink from a passing waitress. As she sidled up to my table I could tell she was at least twenty years older than me, with a lined face and a silver bristled flat top. I had never known a transwoman with a flat top. She was a bona fide MTF stud, or butch, or daddy. A rare species. I was intrigued and little excited.

"Mind if I play?" she asked with a voice raspy from smoking.

"Yes," I replied, "but grab a stick."

We had just started playing 8-ball when she asked, apropos of nothing, "Who's your favorite member of the transgender community?"

"She's between my legs," I said.

"I'd love to meet her," she replied.

I looked at her coyly and said, "I'll introduce you in the ladies room."

This was all unanticipated and moving a little quickly, but I willingly sauntered into the bathroom. She followed me into a stall and said, "Be a good girl and hike up your skirt and pull your panties down."

I did what she asked but was a little nervous, even hiding my girl-cock behind my hands.

"Don't be shy," she said as she put my hand inside her unzipped mechanic's outfit.

She was hard and massive, as massive as a three-inch, estrogen-ravaged cock can be. She gripped my cock and we worked on each other energetically, pulling and stroking until we shot our she-loads, leaving us both sweaty and panting.

When we stepped out of the stall, the young dyke who had wanted to play pool with me was standing there staring at us.

"Can I play?" she asked again.

"No," we replied in unison. As we left the bathroom she gave us the death stare.

My flat top MTF daddy and I decided to get out of the pool hall and continue what we'd started. I was still excited as we walked outside. I got on my motorcycle, first putting on some lip gloss before following her vintage Corvette to her place. We drove west up Fell Street, running into a blur of fog. We parked across from the Panhandle, next to a big white acacia tree shaking in the wind.

She lived in a Victorian flat, and once inside we wasted no time on talk and began kissing and groping each other. I was getting hard in my panties when abruptly she stopped.

"Wait here," she said, walking out of the room. "I'll just be a minute."

I looked around the apartment that was modestly furnished with photos of Formula One drivers on the walls. I looked at her furniture and photos several times over waiting for her. The next fifteen minutes felt like an hour. I was still anticipating hot sex and had maintained that special feeling in my panties. Finally she called out from the back of the apartment.

"Okay, I'm ready," she said. I walked down the narrow hallway to the room her voice had come from.

I had learned to be prepared for surprises, both pleasant and unpleasant. It went with the territory of being transexual. I never knew how people would react to me, or what rude or absurd comment would come out of their mouths. So as I stepped into the room I admit I wasn't prepared for what I saw. I caught my breath and suddenly felt as if I was not in the place I thought I was, being completely caught off-guard at the sight of my sexy she-stud bouncing up and down in the largest Jolly Jumper I had ever seen. For the uninitiated, a Jolly Jumper is a safety swing for toddlers, comprised of a bucket seat suspended from a door frame by ropes which allow youngsters (ages 1-3 years) hours of enjoyment hopping up and down and up and down.

I wasn't sad but I was disappointed as I looked around the room decorated with much care as a child's nursery, only with an adult-size crib and a table filled with giant pacifiers and lots of stuffed animals. I went instantly soft. When it comes to kink, I don't like surprises.

She was naked except for a baby bonnet, a large diaper, and size 13 booties. She was sucking her thumb. Talk about regression. Looking at her I wondered where the hot butch I had wanted to give a lap dance to had gone. I stood there for a long moment speechless. Finally, she broke the awkward silence.

"Don't look so stunned," she said. "The Jolly Jumper gets me in the mood for ass play."

"I'm already in the mood," I said.

She countered, "No Jolly Jumper, no ass play."

I felt bad then knowing neither of us was going to get what we wanted. She wanted me to play "mommy" which I had done many times but right then I was in no mood to fake maternal instincts. I had hoped for good old-fashioned bump and grind primate sex between consenting adults.

Silence invaded the room again, with me standing there confused, and her bouncing up and down looking like she was ready to be breast-fed. Never had I felt so unsexy at the thought of someone sucking on my tits. This time I broke the silence. "Tonight I can't," I said.

"C'mon, I'll give you $50 for a few minutes of mommy and infant bonding," she said.

"No, keep your money," I said, as gently as I could. I lit a cigarette and blew a perfect smoke ring. "Would you like a cigarette?" I asked, then added, "or perhaps a pacifier?"

"A cigarette please," she replied. She took off her bonnet and awkwardly climbed out of the Jolly Jumper. "You'd make a very pretty blonde mommy," she said.

"Thanks," I replied," but I don't want the stretch marks."

She walked me to her front door. "Maybe some other time?" she asked.

"Maybe," I replied, thinking 'probably not.'

I left her building thinking how fate liked to fuck with people, depriving most of us of what we wanted or needed. I climbed on my bike. The wind was gusty and foggy and my seat was a little damp against my ass. I rode around the corner to a liquor store and bought a bottle of whiskey, a box of diapers, and some jars of baby food. I went back to her place and put them outside her door. I have always been kind.

Daddy Issues
Amos Mac

Firefighter John was not the man in the photograph he had emailed me. I also mentally questioned whether or not he was an actual firefighter. His stocky build, rolling layers of belly, starchy arms, mashed potato cheeks, and short stature gave him the appearance of a hairless Santa Clause reject. Not the typical look for an ax-wielding lifesaver who pulled families from burning buildings. At the same time, I was lying, too. I definitely wasn't named "Tino." I was more than a bit older than 19, and I wasn't an NYU student who needed some "extra cash for my books this semester" as my online ad had coyly stated. I also wasn't into dating men. I mean, unless money was involved. I used sex work as a supplemental income while saving for my double mastectomy. I advertised myself as a flamboyant, pre-op FTM looking to provide "Friendship Services" for a fee. And by "Friendship," I meant fucking. Topping, taking, blowing, or just hanging out with them naked. Almost anything requested, as long as they left an envelope of cash on the pillow at the start of our date.

Survival in New York City, even while living in a more affordable outer borough, was nearly impossible when working a minimum wage job without a trust fund. Slinging overpriced skim lattes to celebrities and their screaming, whining children in the meatpacking district didn't pay my rent but it pretended to. Hustling-and coming up with new ways to do so-was always in the back of my mind. Turn a trick a few times a month, lie my way into a focus research group or two, or possibly selling my ovaries. I haven't been on testosterone for that long so they must still work. Hmmm, what else? Forever refusing to look for a real job... A job that would require me to pull my sagging pants up to my waist and tuck in my shirt was out of the question. It freaked me out and that made my mother cry. I didn't even know where my waist was. I'd rather troll around on Craigslist, post some ads, weed out all the responses that were obviously cops, pick a future "financial donor," and hope for the best. I was a lazy hustler. Not a professional but at least I was always safe, letting my best friend, Kenia, the invisible pimp, know when and where I was while on a call.

"Call the cops if you don't hear back from me in one hour on the dot because it probably means the guy threw me in the Hudson," I'd say in earshot of my John. I was a real clock-watcher, just like with any other job.

"Do you have friends who are FTM, too? Because I have a co-worker who said he'd be interested in trying one. And, sorry, but I don't share." Trying one, like an experimental dessert? Are you serious? Firefighter John was a regular trick by now. He lay across the bed from me, hand on cheek, propping up his head with his elbow on the pillow, legs crossed and body stretched parallel to mine on his side, like a schoolgirl telling secrets at a sleepover. He was inspecting me from across the bed. I was an ongoing research project, something to tell his buddies about. Was I a girl with a moustache to him, leg and stomach hair almost long enough to braid? Or was I a boy with a pussy and flattened tits, saggy from years of binding them close to my chest, a mismatched, teenaged Frankenstein?

We were indulging in what was a common occurrence with my tricks: the post-coital question-and-answer session. "How much is the chest surgery you're saving for? And do you think you will ever be getting the, ugh, um, you know... *theee surgery?*" he asked, gesturing with his hands what I could only assume was what he pictured to be my future, gigantic, doctor-constructed penis.

Ah, the Surgery Question. I'd love to wear a shirt that says, Ask Me About The Surgery, or better yet, get it tattooed across my forehead. The ability for people to throw common regard out the window and to be so candid with a person specifically regarding the subject of genitals had forever left me in awe. But it's fine, really. The Surgery Question had become the center of a never-ending joke between certain trans friends and myself. The Surgery Question was almost exclusively asked by strangers or new acquaintances, and laughing at it was a way to make fun of ourselves and people's obsession with the idea of genitalia making the man or woman. Usually I'd answer The Surgery question with a lie, "Oh, I already got The Surgery, you should see it, I'm fucking HUGE, I paid extra, totally!" But this case was different as I was already naked in front of Firefighter John, and he had already inspected my engorged female anatomy with his eyes, mouth, and stubby fingers.

Firefighter John would email grammatically incorrect love letters telling me how he wanted to caress my body and how the next time we met up I would walk into a room filled with candles, music playing softly in the background. I guessed it would be adult contemporary music. He'd write that I'd enter the bedroom and fall into his strong firefighter arms and I would be safe because I was with Daddy now and he'd take care of me. The reality of the situation was far from this. Meeting up in front of the pastry shop around the corner from the hourly hotel I used on the regular, I would see his shifty eyes coming a half a block away. He would always refuse to acknowledge my existence at first and I'd stand there on the corner fake-talking into my cell phone with a bright red baseball hat on. The red hat, representing the red rose in the lapel of the suit I wasn't wearing, sat on my head turned slightly to the side, or maybe it was on backwards. I was always on time; he was always sketched out. He would cross the street two more times, staring at the ground, nervously buying things from the bodega across the street and then right back into the pastry shop to get a bear claw. Then finally his eyes would connect with mine, I'd raise my eyebrows, and we'd walk next to each other down the street, around the corner. He'd pay for a room in the hotel, and I'd walk past the front desk still fake-talking on my phone, meeting him at the end of the hall. He would immediately unlock the door, turn on the lights, and pull down the shades. I'd turn on the television bolted to the wall like the kind they have at the bus station, only here there were just two channels: 24-hour porn or Oprah.

Sex work gigs as an FTM were hard to come by. The majority of guys contacting me hadn't read my ad fully (or maybe they were dyslexic) but they were definitely confused. They would assume I was an MTF, and wanted to know if I was uncut or did I have implants? When I would write back and explain with a photo, they'd write back and ask me if I "dressed up," still assuming I was born with typical male body parts. Suddenly I felt as if my life was centered around teaching Trans 101 to strangers, and it was my duty to educate the masses one John at a time. It was emotionally exhausting, not financially rewarding enough, and I was over it. So one day I dramatically decided that my hustling days were over forever and I quit.

I instantly regretted my resignation. Rent was due in two days and, at this point, I had thrown the saving-for-top-surgery idea on the back burner. I was fucking broke. I needed a miracle but instead of a miracle, I got an idea. I quickly rehired myself as Lazy Hustler Extraordinaire, only this time I'd work it from a different angle. I had heard that fetish and domination sessions with butch-presenting women were a much hotter commodity than FTM escort dates, at least in New York City. It sounded so much easier-not having to explain to every interested party what FTM was and wasn't-and much less stressful. I wasn't a butch woman but I had a woman's body still, slightly morphed from testosterone. I wondered if I would be able to get away with passing as a woman, a reverse transition of sorts?

After placing an ad as a "VERY masculine butch woman with LOTS of body hair" and mentioning vague domination techniques that I would be interested in performing on lucky suitors, the emails rolled in. JACKPOT, I thought. I replaced the hustler name, "Tino," with a more androgynous name, "A.J.," and quickly set up a date for the next day. I'd just hide my trans identity for a moment, put it in my pocket for later, and present myself using the female body that I was born with. I just had to convince myself that I could successfully act butch in front of a trick. I also had to figure out a way to hide the ways in which the past year-and-a-half of taking testosterone changed my body. Shave my teenage boy-looking moustache, that's a given. I can't do much about changing the sound of my deep voice without sounding like a drag queen, so scratch that idea. I made sure not to bind, didn't pack on the way to the date but did pack my harness and dildos in my backpack. Oh shit, what would a butch dom even wear?

I took a piss and then cursed myself: I was on my way to the domination /ass worship / fetish date that was to end with me giving my new trick, Business Trip John, a golden shower. My bladder had been full and I had forgotten why I was holding it in for so long. I pissed without thinking. With an empty bladder, I'd have to start from scratch, drinking everything in sight so I'd be ready to unleash the urine stream on command. I decided on the way to the subway that I'd just make the trick feed me buckets of water for the majority of the session when I wasn't letting him worship my ass or suck my dick. He wanted me to order him around, so why not order him to do something useful?

As I sat on the four train going uptown to meet Business Trip John at the 4-star hotel suite that his company was probably paying for, I caught my reflection in the window across the aisle. Did I pass as a woman just because I shaved my mustache off? I was wearing a big coat, hiding the fact that I wasn't binding for the first time in years. What if I run into friends? Would they be able to see my tits under my jacket? I laughed but felt horrified. What was I doing? I was dressed in tight jeans; intense, too-big, leather boots that my friend Larry and his boyfriend Larry gave me when they moved to that expensive loft in DUMBO; and a tight plain white t-shirt. I left my baseball hat at home and instead played around with my hair, thick and wavy, short but still in need of a cut. I had lathered some product into my hands and played around with the curliness of my mop, made it kind of swirl around the sides of my face. Did this make me look like a girl? Do I still pass as male? Have I ever?

When Business Trip John met me in the lobby of the midtown hotel I was happy to see that he was a big bear of a man with long thick arms, wispy black hairs entangling them like ivy, a full beard, and hair dripping down his neck. I predicted that his naked body would probably be much hairier than mine and this gave me a sense of relief. In the elevator he pressed the button labeled "PENTHOUSE" and we flew thirty stories up. Then he was naked, face first into the furniture, some hideous brown sofa, and I was spanking his ass with my bare hands because he didn't like being spanked with anything else. He whimpered, "Yes, Mistress! Yes, Mistress!" as each slap landed, and I kept swallowing all the giggles that wanted to exit my mouth because I didn't realize he was going to be calling me that.

I turned him around and made him watch me as I put on my dildo and harness. "Come here," I said, and forced him to suck my cock deep until he gagged. I thought about how my girlfriend gave such better blowjobs than this guy.

"Fetch me a glass of water," I barked at him, and he did. I turned him back around with his knees on the sofa again. I put a finger slowly into his ass, then two, when Business Trip John cries, "Mercy, Mistress!" and I roll my eyes.

"Water, please!" I command and he's up again getting me another glass. Tap water, New York City's finest. I'm finally feeling the water back in my system; it's coursing through me and I get excited because I'd never given a golden shower in such a high class hotel before.

I wanted to kill another ten minutes before the grand finale so I tell Business Trip John, "It's time for you to worship my ass and I want it to happen in the master bedroom so let's go, and get me another glass of water while you're up." I lay on my stomach while he crooned at my ass, talking to it, literally. I inspected my fingernails out of boredom and then cursed myself, 'Would a butch dom look at her fingernails like that?' Who cares? Business Trip John wasn't paying any attention to the upper half of my body anyway. He was still conversing with my ass on some other wavelength. I looked around the huge, spacious, top floor penthouse and wondered what company this guy worked for. He had a real job and I wondered what kind... what was his story? I looked at the clock, five minutes left before I was supposed to call Kenia and tell her I wasn't dead in a ditch. But Business Trip John was still chatting away, this time not to my ass, but to me.

"Your ass...," he cooed, "...it reminds me of a young man's ...so hairy and small. And the muscles in your legs are very impressive..."

I got nervous and thought, 'The jig is up, he smells a tranny,' and I ordered him to get into the tub. He lay in the tub like a child and I stood over him straddling either side of the bathtub. The urine streams out of me and splashes down his chest. He's catching it in his hands, rubbing it all over his face, licking his lips, his bellybutton filled with my piss. I was ready to leave.

Business Trip John sat down in the dining room of the penthouse, lit a cigarette, still naked on the hotel furniture. He took a deep drag and watched me as I packed up my belongings and put on my clothing.

"So, A.J., I was wondering... Do you happen to know any female-to-male transexuals that do what you do? Because next time I'm in New York I think I'd like to try one of those out." I told him I was pretty sure I could recommend a certain FTM that I was rather close with, but that I'd have to get back to him.

Free
Megan K. Pickett

I was lying on the couch on a Sunday morning, still wearing the dress but only one of the shoes from the previous night. While half-covered in a comforter that smelled like cat hair and cigarettes, I had my first epiphany about post-transition life. Most people probably do not require this kind of awakening but I've always prided myself on being different. Too bad my father had summed up the lesson years ago, in a different context.

"Son," he said, "there are some kinds of free you just can't afford."

At the time, I thought it was funny, even clever. It was the kind of folksy, fatherly advice that is too often forgotten until just after it would have been a good idea to remember it. Such was the case that morning as I quickly rose from the couch and just as quickly regretted doing so. Once the electric surge of bile shifted back down my throat, I squinted against the hazy, lethally bright sunlight cutting into the room through the vertical blinds. Outside, the steady, hollow bouncing of a basketball accompanied the low, loud bass of a car stereo. I stumbled toward the kitchen for some water and a fistful of Tylenol when my bare foot connected with the half-full glass of red wine next to the couch. This would have been bad enough except that by trying to right myself and prevent the glass from spilling, I stumbled forward, launching the glass with my foot across the room. I watched it propel, spinning dark purple drops across the white carpet until its trajectory was interrupted by the presence of my television. There was a loud thwok! followed by the ringing tinkle of broken glass.

"Goooooaalll!" I shouted to my cat, lifting up my arms, two actions I instantly regretted. To ensure neither the cat nor I would walk on alcohol-soaked broken glass I did some minimal cleaning. I plopped back on the couch with water, pills, and cigarettes.

Smoking is a terrible thing, even more so when you're popping estrogen. Early on, every leg cramp or muscle twinge seemed a certain sign of death by embolism. At the time, smoking was too ingrained in the necessary habits of my day. From the first puff in the morning with coffee to the celebratory smoke following hours of face scraping and burning under the gentle care of my electrologist, cigarettes were always there to comfort me. Even though I had managed to quit in the months leading up to and following SRS (sex reassignment surgery), last night was a fall off the wagon. The relapse brought on by another bad habit, drinking. I needed the perfect smoke to go with the first or perhaps second drink of the night. The problem was by the fourth, fifth or sixth drink, suddenly I had become a smoker again. So there I was... drinking, popping pills, smoking, and vaguely recalling last night.

Usually this is the point in the story where the person you don't remember walks in from the bedroom wearing just a shirt. Then comes the fumbled dialogue and embarrassed glances, the calculation in each mind of how to cut loose. Sorry to disappoint. The truth is that I did meet someone the night before, quite by accident. Or maybe not quite by accident, I don't know. In any case, I made it home without him and thank Christ for that.

It had been maybe two months since my surgeries: a tracheal scrape and a couple of modest implants as added upgrades to the standard model. I was quite pleased with the results but it had been a long time since I had done anything remotely fun as an adult and in the company of other adults. Much of this was self-imposed. I did not want to date until after I had taken care of "The Business"... at least partially. This hiatus from having fun was further lengthened by the fact that my surgeon, the now-retired Dr. Eugene Schrang, preferred to complete SRS in two stages that were separated by at least ten weeks. Since coming home from Schrang's House of Genital Fun, I had been anxious to get out once I was recovered enough. Weeks slogged by and even though I healed pretty quickly, much of those first post-operative days were spent in Vicodin-induced naps on the couch or 'dilating' (a sterile euphemism for shoving a plastic ramrod as far into yourself as possible until, as the good doctor had said, "you can taste it").

Eventually my strength grew as did my displeasure for combining genital calisthenics with watching re-runs of *Law and Order*. My apartment which had once felt capacious and light began to resemble a

91

dark prison, one from which I would never escape. In the end, I resolved to force myself to make a prison break. This is how I ended up at a comedy club in northwestern Indiana.

I had not heard of any of the performers but that did not matter. I cannot say I was sanguine about the possibilities of pseudo-amateur comedy night at the Hoosier Ha-Ha Club. Yet it was important to get out because my other option was spending increasingly large fractions of time barricaded in my carpeted cell.

There was also the germ of an idea, one that sat in a deep, dark corner of my mind: *what if I met someone?* As in *met someone.* It seemed possible. It wasn't that I was desperate for sexual contact with another human being but I freely admit that I missed it. Over the past year or two during my transition about the only action I could expect was when one of my doctors stuck his thumb up my ass during a prostate exam. It was an event that I tried to take, given this view, philosophically.

With prostate examinations being the extent of my intimate contact with men, I was interested in expanding my horizons. Of course, I had no idea what I was doing or even where to begin. In the first place, I had been a guy, and in the second place, back then I had zero interest in other guys. Transitioning seemed to change that. I stress the word "seemed" because even then I was fully aware of my desire to somehow be normal.

At the time this seemed like an admirable goal to just be like everyone else. It seemed that the best way to accomplish that would be through the usual vanilla, heteronormative coupling. Lost in this brilliant analysis was the fact that I was not really your typical vanilla, heteronormative woman. I suppose it's all in the details.

It was all very odd and confusing, I have to admit. As I progressed further into transition I did find some men attractive, something that had never happened before. Looking back I had to ask myself: was I really hot for that guy or did he just fit into a neat, white-picket-fenced narrative? For the record, I do not buy the argument made in some trans circles that HRT (hormone replacement therapy) will set you free in this regard. If HRT could do that then I guess all those years ago you could have just given me a huge booster shot of testosterone. Apart from a thrilling and successful career with the San Francisco Giants, that would have been the end of it. It doesn't seem to work that way. Perhaps it is just the nature of transition with its attendant experimentation and release from years of pent-up repression that allows a person to admit that, in fact, they had been bisexual all along... protestations from certain sex-obsessed psychology professors at Northwestern University notwithstanding. Or maybe you really can fool yourself.

Whatever the reason, I was intensely curious about men and even attracted to a few. So on that August evening, I put on a fairly skimpy, flattering little black dress, my favorite heels, and did and re-did my makeup. A couple of hours later I was ready, so I made my way to the HHH Club.

The first sign of danger was the three-drink minimum. I had not come all this way to be discouraged by a few watered-down cocktails so I went ahead and ordered three cosmopolitans right away. As embarrassing as that sounds, all I can say is that I am a woman of many affectations, and stupid and sweet cocktails were featured prominently at the time. Drinks safely delivered, the lights were lowered and the first of three acts began. The comedian on stage was a strictly local no-talent who specialized in Viagra and gay jokes. The next guy was a little better, somewhat dry in his delivery and humor, but he, too, descended into the usual offensive territory. The last comedian was clearly the best and most polished, much better at dealing with the drunken party seated in front of me. Good as he was, the night seemed to drag on and I began to feel like the odd transwoman out, sitting alone with a basket of stale popcorn and three empty cosmo glasses.

At last the show ended, the lights went up, and we were all herded out of the comedy room and into the larger bar area. Once there, a cover band played songs badly. I needed a beer so I headed for the bar, sat on a stool and ordered. Just one beer, I promised myself and I'll go home, mission accomplished. Except that germ was still there and its light was flickering a little brighter: *Maybe you could meet someone here. No, not for sex, silly. You're not that kind of girl. Well, maybe. Something. Anything.*

"Didja just come from the club?" a voice next to me asked, and immediately my mind went blank. I felt as though I was at that first dance back in junior high, my friends and I clumsily fumbling to the strains of "Rapper's Delight". I turned to see a broad-shouldered man with a neatly shaved head, wearing glasses, and grinning wide with a genuinely disarming smile. I gave him a quick once-over, noting a thick, solid frame which was hard not to notice given how tight his clothes were. When I dallied in being attracted to men I can't say that Arnold Schwarzenegger was my type but as a newly minted woman, who was I to complain?

"Um, yes, just now," I said, quickly swallowing a gulp of beer. My internal alarms were ringing with the fear (like many transwomen, I suppose) that my voice was not feminine enough. As an everyday voice it does the trick, and I do frequently remind myself that there are plenty of women-born-women with smoky voices near enough to mine. He didn't seem to notice anything out of the ordinary, which was good. Interestingly, I didn't give a second's thought about visibly passing. I figured that if he could tell, he didn't care, and if he couldn't then I sure as hell wasn't about to bring it up right away.

We introduced ourselves. He said his name was Hugo. Actually he didn't, but that's the name I'm going with. Not so much to protect his identity but because I have completely forgotten what it actually was. Hugo was a local who ran his own farm equipment business not far from here (a farmer? in Indiana? shocking!). He had been a star fullback or halfback or hunchback at Notre Dame until he blew out his knee during practice. It was sweet the way he tried to impress me.

Hugo ordered another round, which I thought was nice. I began telling him about myself in a general way, letting him know a bit about me without saying something criminally stupid like the digits to my phone number. There was more completely unremarkable talking and a little scooting closer on both our parts. The attention was nice, though I couldn't help but think I did not deserve it. He was nice, but there was something ominous that I couldn't quite put my finger on, until he ordered another round. Somehow, my evening of testing the social waters had turned into a night filled with a considerable number of drinks. I remember thinking (stupidly, I know), a gal could get used to having drinks bought for her, and that's when the bottom of my stomach fell. Though I was not a typical guy in my past, I heard men talk enough. It occurred to me just then that when someone starts buying you drinks, he might think he is entitled to something else later. And if I demurred, what would happen? The possible answer to this question caused a momentary lapse of drunkenness. If Hugo wanted to, he could just beat the living piss out of me and there would not be a damn thing I could do about it. He had not threatened me and had only been kind, though a bit ham-handed in his come-ons. But I could not shake the fear derived from this possible imbalance of power. And what if he found out I was trans? My mouth went dry.

"Hey!" Hugo yelled above the music. "They're playing Petty. You gotta come dance with me!" Now that's kind of odd, I thought, for someone with a bad knee but, hey, modern medicine is a wonder. Believe me, I know.

"I'll be right back," I said, indicating the ladies room. I picked up my bag and started toward the ladies room, then spun around and took a long swig of my beer. I clicked down the hallway toward the bathroom again, turned right instead of left, and hailed a taxi home.

The next morning I sat in my living room, hungover from the drinks at the club and the glass of wine I felt necessary once I returned home. I swore I'd never date men again, such was the extent of the lesson. But of course, I was wrong. Months later, I would try once more to escape my prison. What followed was a series of dates that could be charitably described as disasters. There was Ivan, who insisted on maintaining his liquid diet for our first dinner while singing labor protest songs. Then there was Mark, who wouldn't stop talking about the movie script he was going to sell and the millions that were just around the corner once he quit his job at Quizno's. The other guy, let's just call him "Adolph," sent me emails, sometimes a dozen per night, asking what I was wearing and whether or not I had heard of scat. I suppose it was Adolph to whom I owe the greatest amount of gratitude. He was so vile and awkward that I swore I'd never date men again, again. Sort of.

That Sunday morning I felt dirty, not because I had sold my body for a couple of beers, but because it took an act of cowardice and stupidity for me to learn what a lot of natal women learn just by growing up.

There are some kinds of free you just can't afford.

Made Real
Sassafras Lowrey

There has never been a time that I felt more human, more part of this flesh, than when I am fucking. Society would have us convinced that realness is something that can't be challenged or questioned but if for some reason we don't see ourselves as authentic, we must fix these problems without the assistance of others. My life is not about some self-actualized, pull yourself up by your bootstraps, American dream. This is blood and bone, marrow, arteries, tendons, and I've needed others. As complicated bodies touch, we are molded like soft clay into something resembling a form we can be comfortable enough to live in. Sex is the glue that has held my jigsaw body together. Surrendering to the touch of another has brought me back to self; it's given me back the body I lost to abuse and dysphoria, it has in fact made me real.

I can mark my journey towards embodiment in the memory of my lovers' hands. There has never been a time where my body has felt completely right, but with every orgasm I feel a little more real. Never has there been a moment when my body has felt like my own until I learned to ask and beg to be touched. Sex has given me back my body, taken scorched and damaged flesh and not simply healed it but transformed it. When I have sex it's not insert tab A into slot B, it's not formulaic clean or simple because no aspect of my life ever has been. For me, sexuality is not divorced from gender, it couldn't be. I can't fuck or be fucked without thinking of how my gender plays into what I'm doing. I find nothing hotter than transgressive bodies, and gender is the lubricant I can't ever have enough of.

In my life, gender is a journey, not a destination. When my partner I got together we were both boys. I'd just taken the syringe of testosterone out of my leg and ze was just thinking of starting. Now, nearly half a decade later with me living as a femme, the world sees us as straight. One of many paths on my gender journey, coming out as femme was every bit as gender-transgressive as when I began living my life as a man, even when it isn't seen that way. The hardest thing for me to understand has been the way my gender makes our love invisible. In order to be who I am, I lost being visibly recognizable to my community.

At 17, I began pushing the boundaries of gender, building a community of freaks and outlaws. In order to be queer I had to walk away from family and home. I quickly discovered that there was nothing more radical than love, and learned that holding a lover's hand in public was nothing short of revolutionary. Now, my gender transgression is no longer culturally recognizable, and I miss visibility. I still long for the way revolution was written across my body, the way my flesh was referenced by the world. I miss the recognition of revolution that took place every time I held hir hand. The world sees me and thinks I am nothing more than a straight woman, doesn't see the journey of gender, the effects of hormones still coursing below the surface. When they see hir, they see a straight man, never a butch. Our identities are too complex to be understood in passing glances.

The way we live in our bodies rewrites the pages of history: the stories of our people explain that femmes are made visible when standing next to butches. Our gender transgressions position us outside of that narrative, rendering us invisible to even our own. Hir hand across my flesh brings me home, healing the wounds inflicted by newfound invisibility. Our love is revolutionary, even when others can't see it. Each time ze touches me, hir hands bring more of the pieces of my life together. In hir embrace I have been made real. Through sex I've learned to stop fearing my imperfect body, by fucking I've learned to stay in myself, to resist disassociation. It is through touch that I learned to let go, to trust.

For trans and genderqueer people, our bodies become our battlegrounds, our private revolutions; our genitals, our war zones. We spend so much time seeking survival in our own skin, defending our bodies and ourselves, that when we find a moment of peace it is hard to surrender to that pleasure. As gender warriors we must spend our days being strong, showing any vulnerability is seen as incomprehensible. Our minds, so indoctrinated by narrow definitions of sex, we come to think it's an act which could never include us but as a fag I watched my hands resuscitate boys. Touching elastic and plastic, brining life to manmade objects, I pulled close their bodies and together we birthed new continents, redrew the maps. Topography shifted under our fingers. We altered the course and struck down borders. Through their eyes I've seen Eden. I've witnessed creation, seen self-hatred drown in pleasure, and gazed on as dysphoria dissipated under the realization that body need not be the flesh they were born with, that body need not be made of skin at all.

I've never seen anything more real than the look in my partner's eyes with my mouth around hir silicone cock. Our sex transcends the limits of the flesh. We're doing nothing less than fucking ourselves real. We've created lives and bodies that high school health class curriculums could never cover. In my world, sex defies the laws of physics and constructs new realities. Sex is magic as it liberates and resists being boxed in. As trans people I believe there are few things we can do more liberating than defy the societal norms that frame us as asexual, unlovable beings. We're making families that defy definition, we're fucking with constructed bodies, and we're taking ownership over our flesh.

I was on a service trip doing eco-justice work with a campus ministry when my love of sadomasochism led me, in a roundabout way, into the bed of a Christian straight girl. We spent the days hauling rocks and buckets of soil, trying to minimize the effects of erosion in the Garden of the Gods, a national park comprised of ancient sedimentary beds of red sandstones located in Colorado Springs, Colorado. At night, we slept on the basement floor of a Sunday school classroom not far from the park. Before going to bed, our group of twelve would make the long trek to the local YMCA to wash off the film of sunscreen, bug spray, and gravel dust blanketing our bodies. The scorched asphalt softened under our shoes as we walked down the main drag. Nearing the final day, while on this walk, I got a call informing me of a play party that very night in Denver, about an hour's drive from my park location. Naturally, I was thrilled; play parties were few and far between around my area. I had mentally packed my toy bag when I realized that, because of the commitment I had made to be fully present here for the entire week, I wouldn't be able to return home from the work trip for another two days. Immediately, I was crushed. While on the phone with my friend I tried hard to maintain an even tone to my voice but the excitement and then obvious disappointment showed through. It's not that I wanted to hide my interest in S/M. After all, I was out as a transgender guy and most of my close friends in the ministry were aware of my participation in the leather community. However, there were several people unfamiliar with transgender and queer culture and I didn't want them to feel uneasy or get the wrong impression about me or the communities I was a part of. Plus I wasn't sure that all of my peers would grasp the profoundly spiritual connection I feel while participating in an S/M scene that may involve everything from fire play to flogging.

As we walked, Mel had listened in on my conversation, something that I was utterly unaware of. She appeared to be a typical straight college girl, 20 years old, short brown hair, an impeccable body, and radiant green eyes. Not only was she one of the leaders of the campus ministry but she was also raised by a conservative Christian father. All of my peers, men and women alike, were attracted to this woman. Who wouldn't be? Not only was she gorgeous but she had a stunning personality and a perfect smile. It was no wonder that she was known as the heartbreaker of the group. Word has it that she went through countless men before I entered the picture. From my perspective, there was no chance of a casual fling or a romantic relationship with Mel even though I was more than interested.

"I heard you on the phone," she said coyly.

"Yeah?" I was stuck in my own cocky transboy reality and lost in the fact that I wasn't attending the play party. Furthermore, I didn't think she could really be interested in me or my underground world. Surprisingly, she began to ask me pointed questions about my experiences in the leather community. This threw me for a moment but I rambled on, willing to engage in this somewhat awkward conversation. It was obvious that she was interested. Something had sparked her curiosity. We maintained a flirtatious affinity for each other the rest of the day. If nothing else, I figured that it was nice to flirt with an admired straight girl and have some of that energy reciprocated.

The air was dry and silent as it cooled in the night. My body ached from a week of hard manual labor and my mind was clouded with its own ramblings. I lingered in the space between sleep and consciousness huddled in my blanket when I felt a hand on my back. It moved slowly at first, timid at the touch and cautious in the situation. I didn't know what to do. My body shivered at her caress. I could feel the sexual tension growing, channeling its way through my cells, quickening my breath. I couldn't turn around. I couldn't bear the possibility of rejection or the thought that I had gathered the wrong interpretation from this sequence of events. Internally I struggled, frozen in my skin. Desire spoke heavy, leading me to want to devour her purity in the sanctuary of a 19t h-century church, to drive her to an extremity of spiritual exaltation never witnessed in those pews. In the end, rationality and self-will won out as I disassociated from my being and pretended that her touch was an intense hallucination.

The next day we returned to our normal lives. I assumed that my brush with this woman had come and gone. It was an early May morning about 9 o'clock, less than 24 hours after returning to my natural life, when my phone rang. It was Mel. There was no mention of the previous night; she was planning to get a tattoo and asked if I would accompany her and her best friend for moral support. I wasn't sure what she really wanted. Was I some sexual experiment for her to figure out her own sexual identity? Was she interested in dating me? Did she see me as a good friend, someone to hang-out with, since we had connected so well during the work trip? I quickly understood that each of those questions did not need answering. Without hesitation or the recognition of my own confusion, I agreed to accompany her to the tattoo parlor. Before meeting up with Mel I had spoken with my friend, Lors, who suggested I not get sentimentally attached. "Cam, you could have any queer woman in this community. Why do you always pick straight girls you can't have?"

Maybe she was right. Maybe this woman wouldn't be interested. Perhaps I was fooling myself but my cocksure attitude would not be pushed down. The fact that she was straight made it a bigger challenge.

As the tattooist's needle was placed on Mel's skin, I saw her face exhibit horrendous pain and she reached for me. As I slid my hand out of my pocket to grab hers, our eyes met and she quickly turned away. Perhaps that is when I fell in love. Two hours later, the artist had finished his masterpiece: an elaborate gladiola positioned on Mel's left foot. We celebrated her triumph over artistic pain with Rice Krispy treats and soy chocolate ice cream. Conversation flowed easily between bites of deliciousness. I felt as if we were kindred spirits rejoined after a history of solitude. Several hours later we arrived at Mel's apartment. It was covered with tattered siding, chiseled steps worn by traffic, and beer bottles littering the pavement: the picture of college life. I never expected to be invited in.

"You wanna come in?" she asked suggestively with those astounding green eyes.

"Sure." I was nervous as I entered. In the past, most of the women and men I dated were part of the queer community; they understood the queer meaning of sex, constructed identities, and creative ways of presenting and maneuvering in the world. I've always had an affinity for self-identified straight women but things never seemed to work out.

I was usually used for a one-night stand, sexual exploration or a casual fuck. Often interested in exploring their sexuality, I served as a willing medium but this was something different. I felt out of my zone, much like I did the night that her hand rested on the crest of my back as we slept. She motioned for me to come upstairs. The sexual tension, strong as adhesive, was combined with a sense of confusion and anticipation for both of us.

Once upstairs, it didn't take long for her lips to find their way to mine. I hadn't made the first move, fearing that I might risk my chances at a second date. I wasn't interested in a casual fuck and, if nothing else, I wanted to develop a lasting friendship. As the kissing turned into a full embrace, I pulled away. She wasn't some girl I met at a party or club. I wanted to be careful. As with all my partners, I asked for her consent. I wanted to know that we were engaging in this sexual rendezvous as two consensual adults. In this sequence it was especially important since she was straight. Engaging in queer sex meant a possible challenge to her identity and the entire way she perceived the world. I placed my hands on her shoulders as I spoke.

"Look," I paused for a moment trying to articulate my thoughts, "Mel, if this goes any further I will fuck with your whole sense of identity. I want you to consent to this being fully informed." The utterance barely exited my mouth before she interrupted.

"I can handle that." The words dropped from her lips with striking confidence as she pushed me to the bed. The walls between us crumbled as we fumbled for clothing, pausing only for lips to liberate tender flesh. Mel had no idea of the barriers that many butch women and transmen put up about their bodies, she acted from instinct. Knowing her intentions were pure, I let my guard down. She took little time to remove my shirt, something I rarely did with sexual encounters. My topless, pre-surgically altered chest felt unfamiliar. I shuddered as the air brushed against foreign skin. I could see the hunger in her eyes and for once I felt at home in my skin. What was underneath the layers of cotton did not stop her from seeing me as male. It didn't matter that we came from vastly different worlds socialized in a diverse array of settings. To her, I was a guy, the first guy to bring healing and comfort to her life.

My desire for her was unbelievable; her flesh was startlingly soft. I was gentle, knowing that sex in my world held so many variations and meanings. For me, sex was beyond static definition, created at the very moment of the act. For her, sex had never been enjoyable, mostly consisted of one main position, and lacked a sense of empowerment. I massaged her upper body using my fingertips, palms, nails, lips, tongue, and breath to elevate her senses. We moved in a timed motion, both fully clothed below the waist. I tuned into her essence, every breath became a cue, every movement a point of reaction. Sweat beaded down my back as I pressed my chest into her. My fingers fell on warm hard nipples as our bodies danced together in an intricate motion. I spoke softly, my breath brushing her left ear before my teeth sank into her upper shoulder. Elevated into orgasm without stimulation below the waist, she arched her back and pulled me closer. When she came, she screamed in genuine ecstasy, releasing years of sexual pain and trauma. In her tranquil state she collapsed on my chest, softly humming before drifting off into sweet slumber. I lay there for hours that night, watching her sleep, holding on so tight I thought my arms might fracture.

We have shared so many nights like the first. Each day, her sense of love and compassion for my body and my metamorphosis as a trans guy inspires me to be open about my life and identity. Through this connection we have grown as a couple, labeling my body with words that empower us, such as "dicklit" and "cock-pit" (to represent the anatomy I have below the waist). Yet labels, though helpful in many situations, can bring unique challenges. We have frequently been confronted by the way the world views us. Are we a queer couple or a straight couple? Does this perception depend on the community we are engaging? Do these perceptions even matter?

Like many gender-variant people, my world, gender and beyond, has always been a mesh of identities blended with the nuances associated with them. They are not lone pieces of the self but intermixed with each other. My identity as a guy impacts my connection to the dyke world and my association as a trans fag influences my sense of spiritual wellbeing. My femme, as I often refer to Mel, is similar. To her, these fragments are all interconnected in the perfect puzzle of life; a puzzle that might change shape, color or context periodically. She does not identity as "straight" today as she feels that "queer" captures her essence and the intricately simple life that we share together. Ultimately, my femme has become my source of inspiration. She constantly challenges me and encourages my overall development both mentally and physically. Without an ecumenical, campus ministry, eco-justice service project, I might not have found the queer, masochistic, Christian femme who transformed my life.

Out Loud and Proud Six Months Before Surgery
Dee Ouellette

My name is Dee and I'm a 39-year-old queer tranny woman and mother of a four-year-old boy named Damase. My partner of eight years is a genderqueer bio-woman named Jen and she is Damase's other biological mom. I first came out as trans at the age of 33. I had been seeing Jen for two years at that time. About six months before I came out, Jen and I had been doing some role-playing in our cramped attic bedroom in a North Oakland crusty punk anarchist house. I was wearing a red sequin dress and she was wearing a brown pinstripe suit I had dug up for her in a thrift store. Afterwards she told me, "You know if you ever wanted to spend the rest of your life as a woman that would be fine by me." Oddly enough, that was exactly what I wanted but it still took me a little time to get there.

Coming out as a transwoman was one of the most unique, if not hardest, life experiences I have ever had. Within two years of coming out, I lost a good-paying temp job (where I worked wearing boy drag), lost contact with four out of five members of my nuclear family (it's now down to two out of five), and a bunch of "friends." One thing I did not lose was my partner. That's not to say that everything was peaches and roses in our relationship because it wasn't but we've kept it together through a hundred obstacles. We also have an amazing and diverse community of support and we're thankful for that.

There is no celebration when you come out as trans. The world does not say "Excellent! Another tranny! Y'all are sexy and unique! You should be who you feel you are! Thanks for coming out!" You can't sashay down to the corporate bookstore and decide among titles like *Now You're Out As a Transwoman: Welcome to Hot Queer Sex*, or *Keeping Sexual Intimacy Alive and Well During Transition*, or *Navigating Hormones, Surgery, Parenting, and Polyamory for the Recently Out*. It's just not like that.

We got pregnant in June 2003, the same month we had our

commitment ceremony, in the long tradition of queer potluck weddings. It was early on in my transition, so early on I wasn't sure I wanted or needed hormones but I was certain I wanted to start a family. At the time, I would have benefited greatly from supportive counseling with no strings attached. That counseling never occurred because I was very vulnerable, and my partner and I didn't want to insert a possibly untrustworthy stranger into our process of becoming parents.

Damase was born purple on February 22, 2004 in the presence of our two midwives and three of the four women who married us. A couple of weeks after the birth I made contact with a surgeon in Philadelphia who did not require a doctor's letter for an orchiectomy (surgical removal of the testicles). In August 2004, under local anesthesia, I watched a surgeon cut off my balls and place them in a medical waste container, and I felt happy. Feeling my testosterone level permanently dropping 95% I count among the best experiences of my life. I think it is safe to say that I am not a mole for the patriarchy.

We took Damase, now four years old, to Pride this year and marched with our family's contingent. It was so powerful to experience people of all shapes, colors, and orientations along the parade route crying with joy as we walked by holding hands. Damase was so happy that day, feeling special and finally having a sense of belonging. When we came home, he grabbed a pink T-shirt out of his drawer and put it on.

"What does it say, Mama Dee?" he asked.

I said, "It says, 'Tough Guys Wear Pink'."

He beamed. "Now I have pride so I can wear this." After he put it on, he added, "What's a tough guy?"

You've gotta love our kid.

On my wedding invitation I described myself as a "genderqueer, queer, tranny woman," and I still like that description. It's broad and doesn't play "trans" and "genderqueer" against each other (or "tranny" and "woman," for that matter). Still, it's a little too much identity and not enough politics but it was a wedding invitation. "Genderqueer, queer, tranny, woman, freedom fighter, organizing for collective liberation from white supremacist, imperialist, patriarchal violence and war" is better (a nod to bell hooks here for naming the system in this clarifying way). "Lesbian" is a harder word. I sometimes use this word but mostly for convenience since people read Jen and me as a lesbian couple. But we both identify as "genderqueer" and she has a highly developed masculine expression (as well as a highly developed femme expression) so the term sadly feels too narrow to describe our experience. "Queer" fits better. "Transexual" and "transgender" are also tricky. Those words feel technical, medical, and clunky but I use both these words for convenience in a similar way that I use "lesbian." People know roughly what the words "transexual" and "transgender" mean, and they can and do bring people a little closer to my reality. Also in are "faggot," "dyke," "trannyfag," "femme," "sissy," "fag," "homo," "gay," and a whole bunch of others. Pride-filled words like "mom," "activist," "organizer," "baker," "sweetheart," "friend," "sex-positive," and "fierce" all attach to me easily.

Living as an out transwoman is hard but it's better than staying in the closet. Discrimination is everywhere. As transpeople, we are targeted by cops, vigilantes, and the criminal injustice system. All too often spaces that should be safe for us exclude us. There is a very strong "stay in the closet or die" message that leads many trans folks to commit suicide rather than come out. I believe the vast majority of us are not yet out and need our support wherever they are, and they are everywhere. The great part of coming out was how my mental health and relationships both improved dramatically. It just looked differently than I imagined it might. It probably will for you, too.

ReSexing Trans
Kai Kohlsdorf

For Joey: Thank you for sharing everything with me,
and for allowing me to share us with the world

Sexual contact is the place where our gender identities are hijacked. It is also the place where the fluidity of our supposedly stable gender and sex constructions is shown most clearly. Why has our society gendered our sexual experiences? For instance, a heterosexually-identified, biologically-born male who wants to receive anal sex from his female partner but is too afraid to ask her to do it because she might think he's gay. Or a biologically-born man who dates men questioning whether dating a transman with a vagina makes him straight. On the flip side, mainstream society is incapable of understanding that a transman who enjoys vaginal sex with his gay male partner is still a transman. They seem to be asking, "Why on earth wouldn't that 'woman' just stay a woman and be hetero? Why be trans?" And even some lesbians wonder whether dating a transwoman counts or they wonder if dating a transman would make them straight. Clearly we attach a lot of our gendered identities to our sexual practices, whether or not they "fit." This is particularly true in the trans community. It is important for us to reclaim our right to our own sexual identities as wide and various as they may be, precisely because we have be de-sexed for so long.

For me, it all comes down to the fucking. The validation and the comfort we can experience in sex, the renaming of a chest or other body part, the ability to communicate and acknowledge a need-what can be touched, what can be fucked, and what is too emotional at a particular moment-allow us to experience our identities in the ways we want and need to. Without that, I know I would be lost. And I suspect others would be, too.

Let me take you into my bedroom to explain. When I have sex with my boyfriend, I am having sex with multiple identities. He is a mother.

He is "Mom" to our daughter, and he's also my "Daddy." We still must work within the social constraints and constructions, roles and power dynamics thrust upon us but we choose how they fit for us and for our happiness. For example, Daddy likes me to fuck him in the ass with my dick. I strap it on, and even while we both know who wins in the "bigger man" contest, he loves to take it with his ass in the air, face down. We navigate his conflicted feelings of wanting to be topped and his fears of losing his masculinity by reaffirming he's Daddy even when I top him. After he cums, he usually asks for validation that I do not think he is any less of a man because he likes sex in certain positions. We get close, we cuddle, and I stroke his male ego a little.

For him, the most affirming act that he's Daddy and that he's male is when I get down on my knees and suck his cock. The fact that I'm an extremely effeminate transmasculine person sucking his cock does not negate my maleness for him. I am still his boy, and there is no question because I'm the submissive one. I'm allowed to get on my knees.

It is really important to me that he feels validated as a man when we have sex. My identity is much more ambiguous, much more genderqueer than his own. I get a kick out of wearing girly lingerie underneath my binder and boxers for him. He loves it, and I love cross-dressing. As a result, I don't want to get my dick sucked because he attaches so much of his maleness to getting his sucked. It's the one act we don't reciprocate and contextualize, redefine, or make work for our identities, which totally works for us. I don't want him on his knees sucking my dick. I know he would never be able to be Daddy in his head for that; even while I can fuck his ass, or fuck his vagina-sucking cock makes him female in his head.

When I fuck his vagina, he often asks if I still see him as a man. I suspect that renaming his vagina would help but we've not managed to decide on a name he likes best yet. I never see him as a woman, and I never could. He simply isn't one.

Flashback to the beginning of our relationship. He went by the same name, but identified as female. I was much more masculine in an attempt to validate my trans-ness. I was struggling with the tranny hierarchy of those who'd had surgery or were taking hormones seeming to be more trans than me. I had started taking T, only to stop and re-examine that decision. We were in opposite places and over the course of our relationship we've sort of flipped about. We had the top war and he won. Now he is searching out surgeries and possibly hormones, and I've decided I don't want to right now. Though I've given up on the idea of always "passing", we both pass decently well when we want to but are still "she" to our child and our families.

In the beginning I could never have penetrated him anally. His dominance was much more important to him because that was the only tangible way he could feel male before identifying as trans. Our sex, in which he is dominant, now serves as validation where it used to serve as his only recourse to himself. As a result, there is now more freedom in what we do. In the beginning, when he had only been identifying publicly as trans for a couple of months, we believed his emotional attachments and problems with sex acts might diminish as he became more comfortable and was more frequently validated as male in other areas of his life. This has absolutely been the case for us. It took our sex, and my acceptance and acknowledgment of his masculinity, for him to come out as trans. As he negotiated what that meant for him, he has changed and may still change again, as I have.

We think it's similar to how I was never comfortable wearing female lingerie when I identified as female. In fact, when I identified as a femme lesbian, I never did. It was too uncomfortable. I wanted to, but not as a woman. My impending butch identity came out of that, even though that felt pretty weird to me, too. It wasn't until I realized that I'm an effeminate man regardless of my "parts" that I really was able to explore my sexuality. Until Joe, I had to be the top. His ability to see me as male even when I squeal, twirl around the living room or suck his cock, clinched it for me. In our relationship, our different masculinities are equally valid.

When we fuck, we often talk to each other and say what we're doing. To an outsider, it probably doesn't match what they see is going on. As opposed to fantasy, it is our changing worldview that allows us to define what we are doing. Renaming, reclaiming, and resexing ourselves has resulted in us deciding together what is and is not a cock, a chest, or a finger. He can have his cock strapped on, fucking my tits, and suddenly my tits are fake, and his dick is real. Because it is.

There's a lot to be learned about how we negotiate our gender identities in our sexual encounters, and starting that conversation seems to be the best first step. What would everyone's sex lives look like if we could openly communicate how we felt, and not feel hindered by gender or sex expectations? I would wager a lot of people would be more sexually fulfilled once they found what they wanted. What if the "freaks" (read: mainstream view of trannies) in the room weren't the only ones who needed and used that conversation-that moment of disclosure-to talk about how they want to be fucked, or how they prefer to be touched, what words they like to be used, if any. The language isn't there yet. Instead of using this as a crutch and a cop-out for lost conversations, we need to put in the long hours to create that language, take the extra uncomfortable step, and share it. What I'm proposing is not easy but it's beneficial for everyone. We all need to be heard. If this open discourse, this transformative communication, exploded into every bedroom, we'd all be a lot safer, and a lot more pleased.

When we claim fucking, we transform it and ourselves.

On Fucking A Drag Queen
Glenn Marla

I just fucked a drag queen. Fucking a drag queen is, for lack of better words, *fierce*. So, how it happened:

I walked by her in a club and she made eyes at me. Not subtle eyes, but a queen's looks aren't usually that subtle. She made me feel like she was the hungry tiger and I was a piece of meat. The whole piece-of-meat feeling is not something that happens to me a lot: I'm a fat, sissy-femme transman who works as a performance artist in the fag bars of New York City nightlife. I fucking loved it. It felt like we were two trannies chasing each other into the night. I lit her cigarette and seduced her with the power of my free drink tickets. I asked the queen if she'd like to come home with me and she said yes. I was thrilled.

I was working the party so it was late by the time I got out of there. I got us a taxi back to my apartment; I am a gentleman, after all. I think she was a little nervous, because even though we knew each other from parties and clubs I had never seen her out of full drag. I had no idea what she looked like underneath it all. She turned to me in the taxi and said "You know this is a wig right?" I looked at the gigantic blonde sculpture on her head and with a slightly drunk yet very suave face, I said, "Yeah, I know it's a wig."

It wasn't only a wig. It was corsets, stockings, girdles, padding, tucking, cinching, and whatever you do to your makeup to still have it looking flawless at 4:30 a.m. I wasn't scared of her drag. We were both creatures of the night, queer, glamorous, fancy, and gritty. On the surface, I knew her story and she knew mine. I was curious about how we were going to get beyond the surface.

When I take my makeup off I still look like me, just with less makeup. I don't do corsets or wigs and I don't feel very sexy in my makeup. So the second I walked through the door I ran to wash my face off. By the time I came out of the bathroom she was already undoing and transforming herself, peeling layers of shimmer from her outfit onto my floor. Here was this person, this queen, and she was beautiful.

She began presenting a whole other story. My room was covered in corsets, boas, beads and shiny sparkles, and underneath it all was this new person. I was excited to touch her and somehow nervous, like neither of us were real. Like when you show your high school boyfriend your real feelings, then somehow you are too vulnerable to have sex, even though you have been having "sex" for months. I'm sure she just took her drag off because that's what she does, that's what you do, but I recognized it as so gorgeous, sexy, giving, and vulnerable. Vulnerability is sexy; taking risks, putting your body in someone else's hands, jumping off that cliff, spreading your legs, even if you're not sure you want to.

I had a goal. It was to give it to her good. I felt like I had something to prove to this queen, but I wasn't totally sure what. When I came from the bathroom I was just my plain, boyish, queer self, feeling sexy in the knowledge I can fuck well. I mean, she came home with me from a club, that's what was supposed to happen, right? We're supposed to have casual sex. I was supposed to fuck her well, really well. I was invested.

Out of the big blonde wig, her hair color surprised me. I didn't expect it to be so dark and long. Once she took off all her drag she was left in a bra and underwear. I was layered in a shirt, undershirt, sports bra, underwear, and boxers. I felt bad that she was so exposed and for some reason I had the overwhelming feeling that I needed to be careful with this one. She wasn't a cunty-ass queen in a nightclub anymore, she wasn't a woman, and she was no girl.

I invited her to my bed, telling her how beautiful she was. I tried to avoid the awkwardness with my responsible dialogue about my boundaries... you know, the stuff they teach you in sex-positive tranny school. I began with, "So... you can't touch my bits, I'm gonna keep my underwear on, and I call it a cock." The language she spoke was faggotry: direct, raw, horny, not about boundaries, feelings, comfort, what you liked, or what felt good. She let me know that she "wasn't that drunk" and I let her know that I wasn't that drunk either.

We kissed each other hard the way faggots do in porn, like our jaw lines and Adams apples might pop right out of our faces, like if we were not careful our lips could bleed and we might swallow each other's heads. She was small but wouldn't let herself become a little femme in my arms which, to be honest, I found annoying. We continued to kiss each other hard and fast, rolling around in my bed. I remembered this one was a pervert. I knew it from hearing the way she would talk in clubs, and it was obvious from the girlish excitement on her face when she saw the floggers and canes hanging in the corner of my bedroom. The foreplay - the activity before I put "it" in - was fast, furious, hard... but also quick and panicked. We didn't know each other. We were sobering up but I didn't want us to turn into the characters we play during the day before falling asleep.

I was enjoying exploring her body but while making out she put her hand down my pants and went for my bits. I grabbed her hand and quickly pulled it out, not even bothering to mention anything, but soon enough I was pulling her feisty little hand out of my pants again. Was she trying to be a smart-ass bottom? Did she want me to beat her? Or did she think she had some tranny magic touch, like, "I have slept with girls like you, boys like you, trannies like you, so I can get you to spread your legs." Well, I wasn't having it. It doesn't go down that way with me. We did the dance of the two tops for a while, which I imagine is a little more exciting then the dance of the two bottoms, until she let me fuck her.

I'm not perfect. I made a whole lot of assumptions about her based on the way she presents her gender. What can I say? She looked the like the kind of girl who'd be really into sucking my cock (but it could have been all the makeup). In my head I constructed a fantasy where she would want to suck my cock and it would be so hard for her to stop, so I would have to slap her face to get her dirty mouth off, pull her by the hair, throw her down, slam her face against the pillow, and fuck the shit out of her. I would want to watch her come harder, harder than she ever has, until she couldn't take it any more. I imagine she's a size queen who I tease for a long time with one finger until she is almost in tears, begging for more. Then I'd put in two fingers, get some lube, and work it until she was so wet, dripping down my elbow. I would make her beg for it, not like the bratty entitled queen she is, but like a nice girl politely asking for more. And I would know she couldn't live without more, without a third finger, then a fourth, and by the time we got that far there is no choice, I am going to put my whole hand inside of her. I want to feel her cunt squeeze around my fist, gripping my wrist hard and not letting go.

Well, it didn't go down like that. I did fuck her, and she did come, and we did fall asleep. But I imagined her as a cock-whore, slutty, power-bottom, and... I'm not sure she was. In fact, she wasn't.

I woke up after a couple of hours; you always get a little less sleep when someone new is in your bed. When I woke up I looked at the stunning creature sleeping beside me, and then at the beautiful drag mess spread out all over my floor. Looking around at the synthetic hair, feathers, and fierce sparkle turned me on again. Let's face it, her drag told the story of our sex much sexier than it had been. I woke her up by licking her cunt; I like waking people up that way. She told me I was skilled.

In This Dungeon All of the Prisoners Are Free to Leave
Cooper Lee Bombardier

I think it was 1998 when I met Zee Knuckles as we were performing in a dank yet magically festive basement... you know, me and the crew of rowdy dyke spoken word and performance artists I was on tour with. At that time I thought of the Olympia queers as busy little beavers, ripe with invention and industry, turning dumpster finds and damp cellars into glorious performance spaces, at least until the cops came.

Lola, our host, was a tall, large, curvaceous queer femme who played the cello and belted out original songs with a soulful voice like the love child of Aretha Franklin and Allison Moyet.

Lola took queerness to the next level. While we artists from San Francisco were busy being ironic and post-queer, Lola was being sincere, political, honest, and full of heart. Every time I heard her draw that bow across the throaty strings of her cello, my gizzard would tighten. On several occasions, I had to fight back tears when she began to sing. In San Francisco everyone watched their favorite bands standing stock still with their arms folded across their chests. Lola exploded this cynical apathy with one low, resonating note from her mouth.

Over a greasy breakfast at Spar's Café the morning after our show, I met Lola's roommate, Zee. Zee was a young tranny boy slouching sulkily in a hardwood booth with headphones on, ignoring us all with his CD player. He dressed like one Laundromat visit up from crusty punk. He had close-shorn thick black hair and big brown eyes fringed with impossibly long eyelashes. He performed his detached sullen pout with lusciously plump lips. Despite everything—the rumored massive breast reduction, the hormones, shaved head—Zee was pretty.

We all bought cigarettes from the tobacco counter at Spar's, because you could. Who doesn't love the romance of an ancient, dark wood interior café with pictures of lumberjacks everywhere, and a tobacco counter to boot? I was hoping to quit after the tour but places like Spar's really resonated with the history and romance of smoking and made it hard to imagine not smoking anymore. I splurged on the more expensive Export A's and Zee mumbled at me, asking to bum one.

Zee and Lola squeezed into our van to join us for the university show in Seattle. I always liked college shows. Not only did we always receive an enthusiastic welcome but I often experienced a strange dichotomy of being elevated in my intellectual stature as the students' innocence was perhaps eroded by our sordid stories. I wondered what my art school years would have been like if I had been exposed to people like us back then.

We drove back to Oly after the show. In the van, Zee sat next to me. He nodded off to sleep, jerking awake as his head bobbed forward. Finally, I put an arm around Zee, pulling his head onto my shoulder, and he slept soundly for a while.

I spent a good deal of the endless, cold drive from San Francisco up to Olympia arguing with my friends after telling them that I was trans. I was fighting the inclination to disappear from them emotionally even though I really believe one of the most useful skills a person can hone in life is the ability to exist around folks who make you uncomfortable. My friends loved me, I could tell; I could see it in their eyes even when they were saying, "Well, I think it's just more radical to walk the line in between...," or "I will always love you... but I just don't like men!"

With sadness I realized that, as a female, I could be as masculine and as male-identified as I could possibly be, and that I would be accepted by my beloved dyke artist friends. But if I dared cross that line and slip from symbolizing some kind of butch heroism into the dreaded unknown of manhood, there would be loss and exclusion. As a butch dyke, I would be wanted and respected but as a man, I would be redundant and unnecessary. I could painfully strap down my tits as I did every day for eight years and posture a macho swagger but if I wanted to get the dreaded breasts cut off or grow real sideburns, I would no longer be a known entity to the only people who had ever felt like home to me. It felt like it was an awful choice to have to make.

As we neared Olympia, Zee Knuckles awoke and lifted his head off of my shoulder. In the dark of the van, as if we were totally alone, he looked at me and said, "So, are you totally a straight guy, or what?"

I felt flustered by his forthrightness and stammered that yeah, pretty much I was a straight guy. "I like the ladies, ya know?" Zee shrugged and laid his fuzzy head back down on my shoulder.

We pulled up in front of Zee and Lola's house. They said goodbye to us and marched up the stairs to their flat. A wild urge hit my stomach and I lied to my traveling companions, saying that I needed to piss. I dashed up the stairs two at a time and caught up with Zee at the top. When I breathlessly said his name, he turned around and my mouth collided with his soft red pillow lips. His tongue found its way into my mouth and my hands used his ass like a handle to pull him into my hips. It was a phenomenal kiss, the kind you remember always, the kind that reverberates in every cell of your body. When I finally pulled away from his mouth, I said, "Van's leavin'."

Zee faced me, palms out at arm's length, with a pained look on his face. "Dude, c'mon? You're killin' me. Damn," he pleaded.

We kissed for a second more. I turned, jogged down the stairs and got into the van, dozing off to sleep on the long ride back to San Francisco with a smile as I remembered the feel of Zee's lush lips on my mouth.

Here, living below daylight or simply without it, the walls are red with black trim or dark blue with gold. The kind of paint job that looks fantastic at night by candlelight during parties but alone in the morning you just want to go outside. Outside, driven by a profound need for vitamin D and clean water, the kind that thunders fresh through mountains, the kind they want you to believe was captured in that small plastic bottle you purchased for two dollars and are now clutching preciously in your paw.

There is a certain joy in knowing hardly anyone here. There's something about parties that happen in dungeons or sex clubs that makes sex seem like the most depressing thing on earth despite that hungry, teenaged, almost violent anticipation hanging in the air of wanting sex to happen, ugly or not.

Intermittently I would get short emails from Zee, demanding more of my energy than I had to give. They were always sort of bratty in tone, and the trials and dramas of my day-to-day life left me with little to give to Zee's teasing pokes for attention. After some time, the emails stopped. Then there were rumors.

Once in a while I would hear things. "Oh my god, you remember that tranny kid, Zee from Olympia? I heard he was living as a woman again!" I heard lots of things, things I wasn't trying to hear. Gossip is like that. Don't you feel like you "know" things about folks you never even had a conversation with, just because the rumors were flying around you, getting stuck in your head like bad music in a department store? First, it was that Zee was living as a woman again, stopping hormones. Then it was that Zee was in Chicago and was straight, dating guys. Then, Zee Knuckles was strung out, a junkie, or a cokehead, depending on who was telling the gossip. Then, it was that Zee was turning tricks to support the habit. Never once was one of these stories told in a way that gave any indication whatsoever that the teller cared at all about Zee's well-being. It was just fodder, a shocking story to tell that could take the focus away from the bullshit we weren't dealing with in our own lives. There was such a lack of care for Zee in this gossip that I never paid any attention to it. Or at least tried not to.

After shaking you down for some whiskey I am ready for it, ready for anything. All of the men in skirts dotingly follow you around like altar boys. It seems important to not want your attention; the only way to stand out in this crowd is to feign aloofness while feeling you across the room wherever you are; we are both positive ends of magnets. So I just make a point of introducing myself to and conversing with single awkward men-clients who surprise me when I discover I like them. It's that karmic one-two combo punch when you're being a judgmental asshole and God punishes you with love. You don't notice me noticing you checking yourself out too often in a mirror. I don't blame you; you look good, real good. You are an arachnid in your stilettos with throwing daggers strapped to each thigh, resting above the lip of your stockings. You are like an action figure; you are an insect secure inside this black patent leather exoskeleton.

At one point, a self-proclaimed Marquis who looks like George Hamilton in Love at First Bite *stands over his slave as she writhes on the living room floor with another woman, and I stand behind you as you watch the women tongue each other, and you lean your superhero figure back into my chest, and I wrap my arms around you. I think you are melting into my arms but I realize that you are simply passing out on me.*

About five years later, I end up in Chicago for work. I was driving a truck from Santa Fe galleries to a huge art expo in Chicago filled with half a million dollars' worth of artwork. I asked Lola, who was now living there in a basement apartment below a palm reader, if I could crash with her for a couple days. When I arrived at her place, there was a warm and joyous potluck dinner happening filled with trans guys and dykes and queers of all stripes playing games and music and passing a hat to raise some gas money for Lola's upcoming tour. While I sat on the low, broken-down sofa wolfing down a bowl of some sort of delicious, anarchist, vegetarian deliciousness, I noticed a figure dressed in black appear at the basement door, peer in the window, turn and disappear down the little alleyway between Sister Rosa's Futures Told in Your Hand and the adjacent apartment building. Suddenly I remembered one of the old rumors about Zee Knuckles was that he, now she, was living in Chicago with his/her old roommate Lola! I asked Lola about Zee after a little while.

"Yeah, Zee is going by Maria now, and, yeah, she is living here. She just got home from work and I forgot to tell her we were having this gathering today so she was kinda overwhelmed when saw all these people here. She went in the back door."

I waited for what seemed like the longest hour with this strange feeling of anticipation and apprehension and longing. Finally I asked Lola, "Can I see Zee, uh, Maria now?"

Lola said she was in her room, pointed to a door. "Just knock," Lola said to me over her shoulder and resumed her story to a friend.

Zee/Maria said, "Yeah?" when I knocked, and I slowly opened the door and peered in. Maria was sitting on her bed wearing Adidas track pants and an old punk t-shirt. Her really long black hair was wet from the shower and she was combing it.

"Oh, hey, it's you!" she said softly. She looked away and then down at her feet. She seemed like if there was somewhere to run, she would have.

"Can I come in?" I asked. Maria nodded shyly. I came in and pushed the door but didn't close it all the way. I didn't want to contribute to her obvious feeling of being trapped. "Uh, I can leave, you know, if you want me to" I said quietly.

Maria's head snapped up from her close inspection of her toenails, and she said, "What? Oh, no, it's okay, sit down." She gestured to the twin bed she was sitting on, the only place to sit in her small room besides the floor. Even though it was tiny and modest, the room still felt sensuous and full of mystery. There were dark red scarves thrown over the lamps, giving off an opium den glow. A votive candle flickered on a dresser with a 1920s vanity mirror, the flame made the Virgin Mary dance in its glow. Music was playing softly in the background, something dark and sexy, maybe Radiohead. Pictures hung on the walls, strange collages of nude women Maria made with cosmetic ad oversized lips superimposed over black and white models. I noticed a set of wrist cuffs peeking out between the headboard of her bed and the mattress. I love femme bedrooms.

But most of the night you ignore me because you think I'll be there waiting for you, at the end when everyone else has gone home. I laugh at myself when I am but by then you are passed out and I am lying beside you fully clothed, boots and all. Awake, listening to your thick, slow breathing cascading into snoring and smoothing back out again, struck with an epiphany that I have been here before. Not with you but at least one other, and back then I felt grateful to lie beside the passed-out form of a woman I found beautiful, like some large and loyal dog kept close for warmth and protection. But that was a long time ago and now I am just careful not to want anything. I peeled your drunk ass out of your black leather shell so you can breathe, your body visibly expanded with oxygen before you passed out.

Maria told me that she was afraid of seeing me, afraid I wouldn't accept her. "It's hard to see people from back then." I put my hand on her shoulder. I could smell her hair and her light musky perfume. She looked up at me through those impossibly thick eyelashes, and I smiled.

"Maria, I am the last person who is gonna judge you for your gender expression, you know?" We talked for a while about the last few years, and about some mutual friends. I mentioned the gossip and that I didn't pay much attention to it.

"Well, some of it is grounded in truth, I guess. The first couple of years here were bad. I was in a relationship with this guy. It was bad news. I was using a lot. Now I am working in this dungeon as a dom but the owners make us sub ,too, sometimes. I don't like it but the money is too good to pass up. I got clean and stopped hanging out with my ex and his friends. I moved in with Lola. Things are better now."

Later that night we all gathered in the living room and played Mafia. Maria Zee was hilarious, sarcastic and witty, much more vocal than I remembered her being. She was less shy in front of the group. I sat on the couch. At some point she leaned back against my legs from where she was sitting on the floor. I swore I could feel electricity run up my legs with each breath she took. Her scent wafted up to my nostrils. I had to resist leaning down to put my nose into her shimmering black hair and overdose on her delicious smell. I was hyper-conscious of the curve of her big ass against my boot. Eventually everyone left, and she and I sat in the living room talking until 2 a.m.

"I am going to bed," she yawned. "You can stay on the couch or sleep with me." She got up without waiting for an answer. I followed her, curled up in her tiny bed with her. Her ass pushed into my crotch when I spooned her.

"Maria."

"Mmm-hmmm," she mumbled.

"Look, I want you. Bad. And I am in a relationship with this girl who cheats on me all the time, with people I am friends with even. But I don't want to be that guy, even if she is a total asshole to me, you know? I wish it was different but I can't do that."

Maria rolled over and kissed my eyebrow. She turned back over and was snoring in two minutes. I lay in the dark, my right arm falling asleep under her, my groin pounding with longing so hard I felt I could hear my pulse in my eardrums.

Maria went to work at the dungeon in the morning, and woke me up with a phone call, asking me to look up some references to Victorian Sadomasochism in a book of hers; she needed some inspiration for a Victorian schoolteacher scene with a client. We laughed a lot, and then I got ready to leave.

You are inconsistent and sloppy and full of shit but, for some reason, this only exacerbates your big messy heart rather than obscures it. Try to unravel the physics behind this phenomenon: it's like how lightning actually travels from the ground to the sky but visually it looks to be the reverse. You don't deserve my patience but I give it to you regardless. You flit and flicker from branch to branch, a hungry sparrow gathering crumbs of attention. You are so radically different from the last time I saw you that I assume you are using, that you are high.

I am reveling in the freedom of not belonging here, of not belonging to anyone. My best relationship has been with possibility. With potential. Mine or anyone else's. There are no ex-lovers, no one I would rather not see. Just some acquaintances and some new friends and a whole lot of possibility. Did you know that I am hard to know? That I don't always know how to make or keep friends? That I am a loner? That I can be all work and no play? That

I don't know how to fuck without intimacy anymore and, truthfully, I don't know if I would want to. Did you know that when she left she took with her the expansiveness of my heart? I mean, it broke me. I mean, I am broken. The me that followed you, back when you were a boy, up the stairwell to your apartment in Olympia and slammed you with a huge faggot might-as-well-have-fucked-it-was-so-hot kiss, yeah, that guy, sometimes I think he is a ghost. He's so pale and far away, not quite of this world anymore. I was still getting carded for cigarettes even though I was in my early thirties, and like overnight I looked my age, my youthfulness as a mirror or metaphor of the openness of my heart, broken and bringing me seven years shitty luck. And now here I am in your bedroom, powerful because I am not invested in the outcome. For I am just as lost, I am just as fucked and forsaken as you are.

I received a 10-page letter from Maria a few weeks later, telling me of the feelings she had, and always had for me. Telling me that she couldn't remember if she met me in a smoky bar or underwater but that she could never forget that kiss. Telling me that seeing me again was a reminder of her life back when she felt like she could give a shit about herself or anyone else, or her art. That it was a reminder that not everyone was out to fuck over everyone else. That seeing me again and remembering those feelings for me reminded her that even she once had that kind of innocence within her. And that she wished we had been able to make love that night.

I am not sure which one of us is better at pretending we are okay. You get angry and indignant when I ask you, saying "I am Fine. I am Fine," while whisking the trail of crumbs you left for me to find you off the sheetless bed with your palm. So, no, I don't know what it means to be in your bed, so, tell me -if you even know: do you know what it means to have me in your bed? It means I believed you, at least a little bit, even if you didn't expect me to. Explicate each refrain, hide your face in the pillow, lower your eyes to hide from mine and tell me, what does it mean to be in your bed? Like you, I don't remember if I met you in a smoky bar or underwater. I don't remember much about my life back when hope out-tipped the scales to hurt. Been-there-done-that makes things like tenderness or intimacy radical acts of sexuality coming through the other side. So tell me. Tell me the story of how you met me-I'd rather it be interesting than truthful if there has to be a choice.

I hid the letter from my cheating girlfriend who I stayed with even though I knew she was fucking my good buddy. I stayed with her even through all of the lying and cheating bullshit. Deep down I was terrified that because I started hormones and finally chose to take this path, no one would ever want me again. Some part of me believed that I would be unlovable and that being with a lying, friend-fucking woman was the best I could do. Maria Zee's letter felt like a life-line in that loneliness. It felt like a mirror from someone who understood my journey and who felt just as alone and confused. Maria was a fucking disaster in many ways but unlike my girlfriend, at least she was transparent and honest about it. She never tried to pretend to be anything different. I read her letter over and over, and when I had an opportunity to go to Chicago again, I made plans to see her. I went to perform at a monthly queer performance night, and Maria Zee Knuckles was now living with another friend in a flat that was a true live-work space: it was their apartment/dungeon. Maria said that they would throw a party at the dungeon to help pay my way to Chicago.

Here in your bedroom, with slaves getting ass-fucked on the hardwood floor in your living room, we don't know what it means to lie beside each other. How to negotiate the people we were then with the people we are now, and not knowing being the lowest common denominator. In the dark your room is red, warm and sinewy like the inside of an organ, but by morning, as sunshine and city street noise and the cacophony of a toys-for-tots motorcycle ride assaults your window I will want to drag you out of here. Push you into daylight. Unlike all of the other vampires here I want to give you your blood back.

Within two weeks it will be difficult to ascertain that this ever happened, whatever it is. I will be remembering for the first time in my life sharing a bed with another person who knows empirically how it feels to have body parts that don't belong and ones that may never be there, that every sexual act knocks you against incongruity that you may never carve resolve out of. You unfolded my arms crossed over my bare chest, saying, "Do you think you need to explain that to me?" But you can't take a piece out of the puzzle and still have a picture.

I will be back in the high desert, thirsty, not belonging here either but not knowing where else to go. I will be working on a construction site, placing joists to roof a house, daydreaming of you riding my cock with your thighs tightly around me, my back against the red intestine wall, kissing the thick scars across your chest that trace the map of your journey to male and back again, in between the incessant pounding of the pneumatic nailer I am remembering you out of existence and fucking you into dreams.

On my way to the operating room my teeth were chattering uncontrollably. I could barely put one foot in front of the other. The assumption that I would be under general anesthesia for the C-section I planned that day turned out to be completely false. I was about to have a caesarian while I lay fully awake! It was hard for me to calm down until I fantasized that I was in the hospital having been injured in an actual war. I needed something stereotypically masculine to focus on so I could remember where I was as I did the most stereotypically female thing one could do: bear a child.

After gaining control of my jaw, I stopped blanking out from fear and returned to this planet, ready for what was to come. I began to inhabit my more standard, non-gender specific self while I witnessed the birth of my baby.

I asked the staff to not say "It's a — (girl or boy)" but I forgot to mention that to my sister who had just flown in at the last minute. She yelled out, "It's a girl," and was so overjoyed the baby was female. I'm not opposed to calling males "he" and females "she" until otherwise requested but I don't think it's the best first words to say about, or to, a baby. I mean, what if it's intersex?

Though the surgery was intense and there were complications, I can say that I'm truly glad I was awake to experience my child's birth. Her bright eyes looking at me from across the room was enough to rekindle my faith in humanity. My baby, who barely cried and was so full love, came to me healthy and sound. Though I may always be curious about what a vaginal birth would have been like—maybe I would find myself, maybe I would lose my mind—I was not willing to take the risk of finding out, so I scheduled a C-section.

It was impossible to terminate my baby. I could feel it right away attaching, expanding, pushing, and pulling in an area of my body that I had never felt before. Since I was 18 and realized I was male-identified, I have always felt my chest and uterus were wrong for my body, and I still feel that way, except now I am thankful for what a beautiful human has come from them. Part of me believed I would become a woman, or feel ok with being female after the process of having a child. That didn't happen but I'm delighted to be a father.

Though I am pro-choice, I didn't feel I had a choice with this pregnancy. I was pregnant once before and felt nothing. This time the spirit was so strong I felt it immediately. I felt it in the underground construction site that my friend, the father, and I were sleeping in even before the conception. I told him, "Don't worry, I can't get pregnant," and I knew it might not be true.

My friend was a beautiful street kid who was very precious to me. He was 18, spoke mostly French, and was one of the top fencing champions when he was 14 before getting into all kinds of trouble and going into juvenile hall. I believed he knew everything I was thinking and feeling. I believed we became one person. He was femme and fierce, I was butch and gentle. Everywhere we went people noticed his good energy and resilience. They often gave us money and things we needed to survive. When the construction workers came in every morning, they smiled at us as we gathered our stuff. Nobody gay-bashed us. Shopkeepers would blatantly ignore me as I took what I needed for my baby and me. It was a very special time. The world seemed so perfect that I was sure it must have been on pause for us. I ended up having to leave my friend to stay sober, though one day I hope to find him again. I will always truly love him. My heart is stubborn like that.

I have always considered family an important component to my life. I have been homeless on and off since birth and have not lived with a parent since I was very young. Both of my parents are often homeless and even when they weren't, I have never lived with my father so being a father was all new to me. Unfortunately, I have been continuing my "family tradition" of being perpetually under-housed due to an incredible lack of self-worth handed down from my mother, and the society she was raised in, as well as my own battle with mental illness. At this moment, my kid lives with her grandma but I hope to have her back with me soon.

Life should not have to be one long test. We should also reap the rewards of our hardships once in a while and feel a sense of accomplishment. Sometimes it's hard not to be too intense when you've had too intense of a life. There's this techno song that a lot of gay Native Americans, including myself, love by Haddaway. The lyrics go, "What is Love? Baby, don't hurt me, don't hurt me no more." It doesn't explain anything about love but it is very moving in its passionately desperate tone. I'm like that, too. I hope. I still love anyone I have ever loved. My heart is stubborn like that.

When I think of love in an unenlightened, overly traditional way, my heart becomes crowded and I begin to think I will never love again. When our stories are taken away by abusive situations, we can become too desperate to create new ones and move so quickly, or can become stagnant and withdrawn, refusing to go on. I am beginning to re-establish a core relationship with myself to help me move away from that kind of thinking. I have been working on this core sense of self. This is something I have needed for years and have constantly given up, but now it is coming naturally. I needed to do all the legwork first.

The best part of being someone like myself who changes a lot is if I don't like what I'm going through, I just have to wait a few minutes until my perspective changes, just like the weather in Texas. These days I'm purging all my grudges towards hateful or ignorant people because I need to let go of them, otherwise they can become a part of me. As for my daughter, she is safe and well, and I'm getting there, too. She is an awesome inspiration.

Getting It Out In Public
Jennie Kermode

Some lesbians consider it indelicate to stare at a woman's legs but I've never been the delicate type. One finds delicacy in odd places these days. The woman at the bar seems well toned, healthy enough, but she sits down in a fragile way that gets me wondering. I buy her a drink; we talk. We discuss her dress, the club, the difficulty in finding gay venues that play punk. She's sitting more comfortably now. She asks me my sign. I make my excuses and leave. This is Glasgow, city of switchblades and industrial decline. I don't need any of that San Francisco bullshit.

What's your sign? Such odd questions we ask in the search for a mate, or at least for a night of hasty passion. I used to enjoy plenty of the latter but it gets harder as one gets older and becomes gradually more aware of the shortcomings of one's own body or perhaps, in my own case, that's the wrong word. Sure, I'm disabled, which puts a few people off, though not as many as you'd think. But there's more than that. I'd been sleeping with women since long before I was legal so you'd think I'd have noticed but I put things down to natural variation. My lovers were too polite, too afraid of their own ignorance, or too inattentive to notice what was eventually made obvious by the complications with my health. It turns out that most women don't have what I possessed. I was twenty-seven before I found out. It made sense of the screwed-up hormone levels and what turned out over time to be a disordered internal anatomy. I don't think of myself as a woman anymore. That, at least, was a relief. It was something I'd never been terribly good at. The thing is, once one describes oneself as intersexed, everybody wants to know the gritty details.

For twenty-seven years I'd been sexually active, never nervous about sexual contact because I didn't realize there was anything to be nervous about. Odd incidents began to make sense. People who had been really interested for a few days of shagging left abruptly after we tried doing something different. Rumors began to fly around that I was some kind of freak, which I dismissed as par for the course if a woman asserts herself. How can one judge what is normal except by starting with oneself? I'd figured it was the rest of the world which must be out of joint.

Once I became aware of being intersexed, things were very different. I noted that something like eighty percent of my sexual partners had been bisexual. Sleeping with bisexuals felt safe enough. At least they weren't likely to have a deep-seated horror of encountering something phallic even if was in an unexpected place and, perhaps, on the wrong person. It's difficult to build relationships on a purely physical basis though every now and again there's no stopping it. Fortunately, the man I've been with for the past two years, himself a transvestite, didn't let his self-identification as "straight" get in the way. It's not a political or social issue for him, just a matter of what he finds attractive. As I've got what he wants, he's happy enough for me to have extra bits, too, and he pays them more attention than most of my previous partners. With the understanding between us that I can expect to function differently from other people, it's easier for me to determine what I want. He never makes me feel that I'm not enough. It's reassuring when he's flirting with women to know that I can give him something they can't.

Ours is an open relationship (I already had another partner when I met him), though neither of us is particularly interested in chasing other people, just open to possibilities. What's difficult is striking a balance. I envy the fact that it's so much easier for him in that what people see (once they've figured out he's male) is what they'll get. I still find plenty of attractive young women flirting with me but it feels as if there's an inordinate amount of stuff to be negotiated before we can get down to it. If they're attracted to me with my clothes on, will they still feel that way when they can see my scars? If they think they've scored with an attractive woman, should I warn them that they're not going to get the deal they expect? Will they want me to provide them with a beginner's guide to intersex conditions? I don't often have the energy for that. I no longer feel right about bluffing it and just letting them find out (or fail to notice) later. Some of them already know. As a writer, my reputation precedes me but that can also prove to be quite odd. Last year I was hit on by a woman who admitted outright that her medical training was a factor in her fascination with my body, which is a bit of a mood killer. I like to think that my partners will relax with me and let me show them a good time, not lie there carefully making mental notes.

I wonder about this attitude towards intersex people. When people discover that my beautiful girlfriend is in fact a man, they don't ask how big his penis is. Although some women are apparently insecure about the comparative size of their inner and outer labia, it's not the sort of thing they can expect to be asked about by a potential suitor. And yet intersexuality, because it's rare and variable, fascinates people like an old Victorian freak show. Once that fascination takes hold, ordinary manners are often forgotten. This is a state of affairs which many intersexed people find deeply distressing and refuse to comment on at all. In fact, it's one of the reasons why most identify as 'intersexed men' or 'intersexed women' rather than as something that breaks the boundaries of those gender categories. It's easier to be a man or a woman with an unusual medical problem, and I don't blame them for that. Personally, though, I'm not so easily unsettled. I've certainly been asked more unpleasant questions in my time and I've been on the receiving end of any number of unsavory suggestions. The problem isn't so much that I deeply resent discussing my body (at least with somebody I'd like to take to bed), but that I don't quite know how to.

Intersex is a fairly new word. Until this century, people like me were usually, misleadingly, known as hermaphrodites. (Properly speaking, a hermaphrodite has both male and female sexual organs; the vast majority of intersexed people do not.) It's nice to have a category even if it covers a wide range of different conditions. In Australia, intersexed people can now be legally recognized as such. However, this is our only word. Assorted pieces of medical terminology describe specific intersex conditions but not in a way that an ordinary member of the public could be expected to understand. What we lack is a suitable vocabulary for naming the non-standard parts of our own bodies. Without this, we are forced to keep referring to genitalia as oversized clitorises, or micropenises, as if we were merely failed men or women and not individuals with physiological, sensual, and sexual stories of our own. Furthermore, the range of intersex conditions is such that some of us have anatomies which are quite difficult to describe in these terms. This makes it difficult to let prospective partners know ahead of time what they might be getting into.

So where do we go from here? Oftentimes I feel angry, an emotion I never used to have. Perhaps anger always stems from insecurity so it's something that simply didn't occur to me when I believed my body fit an accepted type. But it's dangerous to worry about being accepted. I am a firm believer in keeping politics out of the bedroom. Bodies always have their little surprises. Perhaps it gets easier as one gets older: what was once considered imperfection is simply termed "variety."

This year, while trying to find out if I have the potential to become a parent, I underwent bursts of feminizing hormone treatment. These treatments made my illness much worse and, given the circumstances, are too risky to repeat. I have to say that in many ways I was relieved. It gave me a startling insight into how one of the other halves lives, and I shall never again be dismissive of women who protest that they're feeling tearful because of the time of the month. The mood swings were horrific enough but it was the general rise in pitch of all my emotions that disturbed me most. I've always been a passionate person but have never so easily felt moved (even against my will) to feel giddy, or so easily upset. If this is the price of being able to bear children then those brave people who live that way, who keep the population going, have my deepest respect.

The feminizing hormone treatments also did bizarre things to me physically. I've always been a six times a night kind of person, given the chance, and I didn't know what it was to have so little sex drive. I really struggled to get an erection at all. Once every two weeks or so I would achieve an orgasm with a lot of patient help from my partner, but I couldn't ejaculate. There was no discomfort involved in this as there was simply nothing there to come out but, all the same, I felt denied some important psychological release. The physical process of ejaculation has always made me feel refreshed, satiated, like collapsing into a seat after a long run. Without it, sex was very different. It made me wonder about the women I'd met over the years. Did they have a different experience from mine or were male allegations true, that it was really more about relationships for them?

It's a long journey from becoming aware of one's body intellectually to understanding it emotionally. In some ways I'm glad that I had those hormone treatments, unpleasant and damaging though they were, because they've given me something against which I can compare myself. Having a clearer idea of what I'm not, I feel more certain of a comfortable psychological fit with what I am physically. This sense of a solid identity is the first step on the road to asserting that identity with others, including doctors, activists, lovers. This isn't just about coping with meeting new people, it's about being able to participate fully in my existing situation, being a whole person with nothing that I feel I need to apologize for. My partner laughed at the notion that being intersex could have ever put him off but not everyone is that open-minded and it can be difficult to know how things are going to turn out before one tries. Still, I guess one can say that about love in every case.

Unicorn
L. Winterset

The call was unexpected, and the question she broached was even more so.

"Why don't you date women?" she said.

I was on the phone with my best friend from college trying my best to answer her pointed inquiry. I could have summed it all up by saying succinctly, "I'm a trannyfag," but I stuttered, stammered, and blurted answers in run-on sentences. I detailed my rough and painful experiences of dating straight men in my effort to locate the elusive state of "normal" I assumed I would find with them. How would dating women change my identity, my hetero-privilege?

As the last bit of explanation tumbled out of my mouth and her listening patience was at its end point, I finally said, "I'm gay, not like lesbian-gay, like gay-gay. I'm a gay boy." I could not believe I'd actually said it out loud.

I was so afraid of hearing her response to my admission, I could barely breathe. Never mind that she had just finished a theater piece on queer theory and was now making a film on personal experiences with queerness. I still had anxiety associated with this admission. My automatic response was to wait for her condemnation. Within the second it took her to respond, I thought, 'Why did she ask me that question in the first place?' And then I got my answer.

"I'll be a gay boy with you."

I wished she could have seen my smile through the phone. I had just broken up with my last boyfriend because he never believed me when I told him I was a boy. My tranny-self was a tiny flame in my soul, an ill-nurtured and nearly dead part of myself that had almost given up the possibility of coming into being. I tried on a daily basis to convince myself that feeling trans was made up, crazy or stupid but that one sentence she uttered helped change all that. Those words flowed easily off her tongue and fanned the flames of my trans self. It had taken years of failed relationships with heterosexual men to finally find someone: a girl who understood I was a gay boy, and that did nothing to stop her from asking me out!

We never really went on a date. I was so nervous about the implications of dating a woman and so worried about the possibility of losing my best friend that I couldn't bring myself to date her. We just spent ever-increasing amounts of time together until one day we dove in headfirst. The first time I had sex with her, I knew I was truly male. My maleness became all the more apparent knowing she believed in its existence as much as I did.

In the beginning, our relationship consisted mostly of fucking and ordering in Chinese food. Several months later, she suggested we use a strap-on. I tried to play it cool but I trembled with embarrassment when we went into the sex toy store and she picked out a cock and harness with the self-assurance of a pro. Having strap-on sex for the first time was like being a virgin again, everything at awkward angles and lacking in rhythm.

After a while it stopped being uncomfortable. Like a teenager discovering sex for the first time, I became fanatical about using a cock. This was how I began to relate to my sexuality, and I felt years' worth of sexual fear and discomfort start to melt away. She trusted me enough to let me be myself, and that trust finally allowed me to enjoy myself, to open up to her. I trusted her with my pussy. With her, I actually came, over and over again. To be seen as I truly was allowed for love to blossom like never before. I began to make peace with being a gay boy in love with a queer girl.

The first year of our relationship was filled with frequent and passionate sex and then, out of nowhere, something in me shifted. I cannot describe exactly what happened, but sadness overcame me, and sex ended in tears or my refusal for reciprocation. I stopped wanting to be touched. Sometime sex with the strap-on felt so real, I didn't want the illusion to be broken by my girl pointing out with her tongue that I had a pussy. There were times I was so disconnected and numb when we had sex that I would watch with a blank look and a hollow feeling as she came. I couldn't help but be consumed by anger for my missing piece. Its absence was constantly highlighted by the piece of silicone I was wearing and the leather that kept it in place. This feeling reminded me of a fairy tale I knew, of a unicorn that was captured by a magician and put on display. Unicorn horns are invisible to humans and the people who came to see the creature mistook it for a horse. The magician had to put a steel horn on the unicorn so that people could see it for what it truly was.

Even now when I strap on a cock for my girl, I feel confused and sad. The body I have to work with doesn't feel good enough. I hate the idea of strapping something on to replace what biology has kept from me. I have become increasingly focused on her body and her pleasure. It seems the more I focus on her, the less I have to remember the disparities that exist within my own body.

My once beautiful and sacred pussy that used to open so kindly for my girl is fading away. These days, the only way I can come is to fuck her with my silicone cock. But still, thoughts break through and ruin the romantic mood. *Dildos are for lesbians. Why don't I have balls? Why do I feel so plastic when I touch my cock?* After I fuck her, she kindly asks me if I want anything in return. I don't have the heart to tell her that all I want is to come with her, inside her. I end up trying to fall asleep quickly so I can forget.

She has asked me if I want to physically transition, build my missing piece, but I know transitioning doesn't work for me. I'm male but I'm not masculine. I'm a girly-boy, a drag queen, a femme fag. I know that I'm a man and I know that I love presenting as a woman. I love my breasts and squeezing into sequin dresses. I wear wigs because I am acutely aware of my femininity and my female expression being a performance. I am a man. I express myself through female presentation. Taking testosterone and putting binders on, dressing in baggy jeans and baseball caps, feels foreign to me. Having a penis, going to gay bars, and wearing heels and makeup does not. I know what I want and I know that I can't have it. Some days I can't bear the longing of every body part being where it's supposed to be, and not being removable or manufactured and molded. The possibility that some girl down the street could possibly have the same cock and be fucking her girlfriend with it just kills me.

All this confusion makes me all the more grateful to have my girl, my wife. When I am inside her, I can feel her and I know she loves me. She loves me and loves that I am a gay boy and wouldn't have it any other way. And in all honesty, I wouldn't either. As gay as I am, I love that she's a woman. I love it because I know that female is the gender that fits her, that makes her happy, and I would never want to deny her that. She is the first person who has really seen me when they've looked. I love her because she is a woman, not in spite of the fact.

There are days when loving a woman and being a fag collide. Days when I go to gay bars with her and detest that I am being read as a lesbian or fag hag. When my fag friends get hit on, the jealousy swells. Not because I want to be with anyone other than my girl but because I want the offer. I want a gay guy to see me, desire me, and want hot sex with me. I want my fellow drag queens to not see me as a drag king or, god forbid, a faux queen. I want entry into the faggity, sometimes bitchy, circle that is male queerness. Being perceived as a lesbian doesn't help that quest.

When I'm home with my girl, none of that matters. I know she sees me as the gay man I am. She loves me when I am her sexy boyfriend and loves me when I am her drag queen. I know I'm what she wants, she tells me that all the time. She loves genderqueers and she says she loves me best. So for her I strap on my cock to fuck even though I know she doesn't need it to be able to see my unicorn horn.

Give Back
Taylor Xavier

Don't think I don't know that I owe my very existence to women
    like you.
The ones that held us through the night when the shit was
    kicked out of us by the keepers of the keys, the cocksure men
    on the streets, our own brothers.
Don't think I don't know that you are the one that I should be
    praising nightly for the chance to just breathe.
See, I've seen women like you in my dreams,
Watched them walk down the streets, head upright, hips
    swaying, hearts held tight
Women who can hold all the tools necessary to sculpt minds,
    perceptions, and power
Within the compact tucked tightly inside a make-up bag
    a woman, built femme tough
Strong enough for a man, but made for so much more
A woman who walks, talks, and touches with fierceness,
Earned enough calluses to harden her hide
But known the power of exfoliation at just the right time
To let her softness still shine through as her palm rests upon
    your back

Lady, you leave me trembling
My knees shaking as I stand when you walk onto the floor
Cause I know that I'll be at your feet in no time
Watching, waiting for the chance to light your smoke,
Hold that door,
Take your coat,
Your hand,
This dance.

And before you start backing up,
Afraid of the idea that this is all an act,
A measure of chauvinism, as if to say that these are things that
    I as a man must do
Because you as a woman can't,
Let me remind you of the body I walk in.
The modified parts still a mirror of my mother.
As a child, I saw the sadness in her face through the reflection,
The years of struggle etched around her eyes
And watched how she scrubbed off the lipstick traces nightly
Resenting the invasions that they brought
From the ones who tried to remind her just where her place is.
I saw the force that she brought with her
    to every face-off
Bringing the catcalls down, leaving her blood
    at the site of every fight.
Refusing their stolen hold over her.
And when I told her I was taking the girlchild reflection from her
We talked of how alike he and I would look
The man who had violated her the most.
The one who had captured her with her wingback.
And my mother asked me to never treat anyone the way
    that my father had treated her,
Looking into her eyes in that moment and watching
    our line go back sevenfold, requesting just this,
I vowed to her,
That I will show everyone that I am her son.
And that I will make her proud of the love that I will bring to
    those I meet along the road.
So when I hold the door open for you,
It's just that, a token of relief from the harshness, a simple thank
    you for being here,
A gesture of praise.
And besides, anyone that can make a dress look that good,
Deserves all her doors to be opened.

Boys, c'mon, you know the ones I'm talking about
The women who can look you straight in the eye and

Knock the living shit out of you
Until you are left, dumbfounded,
Walking around like a fool with your pants around your ankles.
These are the women we need to be praising.
So if I hear another butch queer in the house
Pass off a femme as just some tuna
To be sought, bought, and canned
Placed on the shelf
Until the market value is just low enough for you to afford
I'm going to wring my mother's wrath around you
I will gather the lost pieces of her rage scattered throughout
    her years
And ram them down your throat until you are gagging and you
    finally acknowledge
The gifts that you have received from
These women, the ones who have brought you here
To the comfort and security to walk down the street, unscathed.
The nurses, the mothers, the keepers, the watchers, the sisters,
    the dreamers, the lovers.
Women like Joan Nestle, Minnie Bruce Pratt, Amber Hollibaugh,
    Michelle Tea, Leslea Newman, Tara Hardy,
    Barbara Cruishank
Until you realize that they aren't just playing dress-up for your
    viewing pleasure
They're doing it for their lives
To live out the raging beauty that is within

So stop puffing out your chests
With your overplayed macho bravado
And stand witness,
Listen to her words, hold her close,
    and give back.

You owe her at least this.
Give back the soothing words she has given you,
The comfort that she has warmed you with,
The bandages she has taken from her heart to place gingerly on
    your wounds,

Give back.
And when her eyes meet yours after a stranger tries to belittle
     her body
Tries to make claim to a fire that they will never be strong
     enough to handle,
Remember the nights that she let down her guard and let you in
Stand up for her
Don't let anyone degrade her,
Especially those that are bound by our struggle,
Speak up when you hear someone trying to invalidate her worth
Because you've been letting her down for far too long.
I've watched you caught up so tightly in your own passing
That you didn't stop to take notice of the pieces of her dignity
Being chipped away by vultures
And how she has resisted the hardening every time in the taking
     back.
Don't you dare let anyone try to cool this fire,
Because she's been fighting to keep it burning strong long before
     you came around.
This isn't about you needing to protect her, she's got that
     covered fine without you.
This is about her needing the respect that you've been shorting
     her on.
As you've tossed aside the allegiance that she has given you,
Playing her off as your chew toy, fetching only when you see fit.
So if she accepts your hand,
Be sure you are worthy of it
And don't back down from her watch
Treat her right, be there for her, prove to her that you are
     bound by honor
To make her days a little bit better
To be the stop at the end of the road for her to unload
Wrap your arms tightly around her
Let her softness sink in,
Hold her closer,
And give back more.

When I was growing up in the early '80s, there was always a sense of 'us vs. them' when it came to my family talking about gays and lesbians. While my mother (who pretty much raised me on her own) wasn't particularly religious, the rest of her family was. I was exposed to the closed-mindedness and snide comments they made about people who were not Caucasian, straight, God-fearing 'folks like us' regardless of how much my mother tried to shield me from them. From being around such close-mindedness I had always known I was different.

Before puberty, when I would go out to buy comic books, music, or role-playing game materials, I would frequently get called "Miss," and was asked what gender I was on a number of occasions. It seemed so unusual and confusing to have strangers use female pronouns for me. It was much later when I realized how much it affected me and how much I liked being perceived as a girl. Shortly before my tenth birthday, I analyzed the situation and knew what was going on: I had a girl's mind but was in a boy's body. My reality was that I was born with a dangly-thing and needed to do whatever it took to prove to myself that I am not a woman and be seen as 'less than.'

Peer pressure gave me the impression that I had to change the way I carried myself in order to become 'a real man.' Much to my disappointment, no amount of practicing created the desired effect, and I ended up being seen as "one of them faggots." Being seen as "one of them faggots" was pretty much pounded in my head by the time I got to high school. (My alma mater had "Farm" in the school name, which should tell you something about my environs). I got used to having "queer" yelled or whispered to me in the hallways, not to mention cussed at, called names, kicked, punched, and beaten up by other men for being different.

During my high school and post-high school life there was a lot of speculation about my true sexual orientation. I stubbornly insisted that I liked women and never gave inkling otherwise, although I had a few gay friends. Inside my mind, the struggle for identity was straining my emotions. I always had to be in a relationship because otherwise it would seem like what little masculinity I had would forever be in question by others if I wasn't with a woman.

My relationship with women in my life as The Boy was a double-edged sword: on one hand, I could identify more with female-bodied folk and was better at conversation and communication than most of those in male body, at least in private. Get me out in public however and suddenly I became an actor. Every nuance of the way I acted in a large group of unfamiliar people was rehearsed. I tried to be as masculine as possible in order to avoid being seen as "one of them faggots." The few times that I was called "Miss" (probably because of my long, dyed, fine-textured hair), I quickly corrected the person and ended up getting annoyed and twitchy afterwards.

I went through three fiancées between the ages of 17 and 22, which speaks volumes about how important it was to not let that mask slip any more than was humanly possible. There was only so much that I could do, however, as quite a bit of my nature and mannerisms was totally out of my hands. One of my girlfriends and I were in the middle of a hot make-out session when she suddenly looked at me curiously for a few minutes. Eventually she said, "You know, you'd make a very pretty drag queen!" Needless to say, I was less than amused about that comment.

By the age of 22, I had enough of hiding and lying to myself. My former stepfather passing away made me truly think about my life. Could I picture myself being happily married to a woman and having kids as a man? No, I wanted my body to reflect what I felt was the true me, and the wanting marriage and kids didn't have any bearing on it. So in 1996, I came out to everyone for the first time in my life. Most of my friends were accepting, as by my early 20s most of the people I hung out with had settled down in their stereotypes of human beings. In private, other women would refer to me as "Kate" (the feminine version of the nickname I was using at that point) and use feminine pronouns in relation to me.

Around that time, a close female bisexual friend and I made a stab at a relationship but it was like kissing a relative and didn't last. The one boyfriend I had lasted all of ten days before he stated he wanted a 'real woman.' He couldn't understand why I could possibly be upset about that comment.

I then moved to Boston and saw the city as a possible starting place for me to do something about my gender identity but I fell back on the dream of getting married and having kids and didn't press forward with it. Interestingly, the girlfriend that I had was open about dating me despite knowing that I wanted to transition. She gave me what I call the Best of Both Worlds line, which runs along the lines of, "Well, hanging out with you is like hanging out with a girlfriend but having sex with you is like being with a boy." I was less than amused by this comment as well.

It wasn't until late 2000 that I seriously started trying to find some help for my gender issues. What put me over the edge was meeting and living with my father, stepmother, and half-sisters. I spent a lot of time with my sisters who looked like me, acted like me, and shared some interests with me but they were definitely female. Part of me thought, "So that's what I would look like." I finally got the nerve to let them know my true feelings. The reaction from my father's family was apocalyptic; I was told to move out a few weeks after an epic argument between me and my stepmother and father about wanting to pursue transition. Where I had expected support from caring family members, all I got from them was how I was more like my mother, who they generally perceived as evil. Eventually, his family disowned me and made up lies to cover up their feelings about what I wanted to make of my life.

Admitting that I really was female, at least mentally, brought about quite a few issues within me. I figured that since I wanted to be perceived as such, it probably meant that I had to be attracted to men instead of women. The thought made me retch but I figured, "What the hell? May as well give it a try." Needless to say, after two attempts at losing my version of virginity (one of them tried to slip it in, like I wouldn't have noticed) I gave dating men up as a bad concept. I could be attracted to men, but couldn't bring myself to do anything sexually with them.

But how could I date women if I was one? The thought of me identifying as lesbian was a laugh at first; the stereotypical frat-boy joke about how a man would give anything to be a lesbian. It seemed like something out of Jerry Springer. It also subconsciously reeked of memories of my childhood where 'they' (i.e., gay and lesbian folk) were considered deviants, repulsive, and sick individuals. I can't be like that... can I?

Around this time, I had a natal female acquaintance who tried to teach me about being a woman. She was a gorgeous redhead who seemed to carry an air of arrogance about her wherever she went. She was someone who really helped me buckle down and begin to master the superficial things about appearance and demeanor that eventually helped me blend in. She also enabled me to realize that I didn't want to be the same type of woman that she was. I didn't want to be flashy, a goddess, drag-queenesque, or anything highly glamorous. I just wanted to be me. When the group of friends that I had through her disavowed me, I turned to the only other group of people that I thought might be okay with me, the queer community.

The good thing about getting involved in the queer community was that I was able to network with other transgender women, and begin to realize that women come in all shapes, sizes, forms, and orientations. It still took me years to feel okay about my identity as a lesbian but that was when the germ of the idea started. I flirted with quite a few people but didn't have any major moments at that point. One female-bodied person I flirted with and crushed on eventually went on to transition to become male-bodied, while a lesbian couple that I was friends with took me in when I became unemployed.

Eventually, I moved back in with my mother and teenage twin brothers. I knew my mom wanted to keep an eye on me and, to a certain degree, make sure that I was mentally okay. I went through my first serious lesbian relationship, an eating disorder, self-image issues, and so much more under my mom's roof, and she was able to give me as much guidance as she could. The better part of learning what female has really meant to me has come from my mother.

After relocating to Saint Louis from the suburb that my family had been in, I started working as an Administrative Assistant at a local church, which is ironic since technically I'm not Christian and living my life as a woman. In the present day; I generally blend in (I don't like the term "pass" because that insinuates that there is also a "fail," which is a misnomer) and went from receiving shit from the lesbian community for being transgender to generally being accepted as just another dyke. I don't feel shame in my having transitioned however, and jokingly refer to myself as a 'Tranny Dyke.'

One of the biggest changes in my life that occurred after transition was my feelings toward sex. Before transition, sex was more or less mechanical, although I eventually got good at performing oral on my girlfriends and it was easy for me to attain orgasm. I imagine that many of my girlfriends were frustrated about the lack of consideration I had for their wanting to have orgasms. Being raised male, I wasn't sensitized to the sexual needs of women. I was taught that, as a man, my satisfaction was all that mattered when it comes to sex and women can take care of themselves if they want to. This was clearly a heterocentric view on the issue and I had a lot to learn. Sex now is more than I ever could have dreamed about. I still find it somewhat unbelievable that my body feels to my girlfriend the way that hers does to me. Although I'm still pre-op, I have no qualms about utilizing my genitalia (I call my girldick "LuAnn" for no real reason) when me and my partner want to. I don't feel disgust for my genitalia anymore, though I dislike what it represents in society's eyes. But society won't know what I have in my pants from looking at me unless they peer at my driver's license or medical records. While sex is not necessarily the be-all and end-all to a relationship, when your body becomes a closer expression to who you feel yourself to be, being in your body and expressing that being through sex can become quite an awesome sensation as you become attuned to your own concept of sensuality and sexuality.

Ultimately, I've learned that there is no shame in being who I am: a queer transgender woman. I have learned this for myself and can now be satisfied in my life. I know that my viewpoint about anything—sex, gender, relationships or even existence—is not the only one that matters. Being open to others' experiences in life has been what has gotten me this far and has helped me to grow as a human being. My hope is that people will give me the same kind-hearted open-mindedness back.

On Not Fucking or Running in Huê
Aren Z. Aizura

Under a bridge in central Vietnam I'm about to suck Hoa's cock.
He's leaning against a concrete pylon and I'm swatting his hands away
from my fly with my left hand. My other hand pushes into his cheek,
pushing his head back so I can suck at the stubbly skin at his Adam's
apple.

I didn't mean to get this toppy, I just don't know what else to do.
He seems to be okay with it though. He grunts as I cup his balls through
his jeans. I'm crazy hard and wet, too, but I'm not thinking about myself.
Pressing his wrist to the gritty coldness of the pylon, I kneel and unzip
his fly. Rocks dig into my knees and ankles. It's dark and I can hardly
see the shadow of his erect cock, the tent it makes in his underwear.
But seeing doesn't matter. Tasting matters. I suckle on him through
the dry cotton. He smells musty with a tang of salt. When I get to his
naked cock, I try to go slow. I milk saliva into my mouth, tongue sucking
against my bottom lip. He pushes against my face and I push back with
my palms against his belly and thighs. I lick his foreskin and slide my
mouth down, just glancing off the surface of his penis. When his cock
is deep in my throat I reach for his hands and guide them to my head.
It's like the signal he was waiting for. He fucks my face hard. Now I'm
rubbing at my own cock with one hand but I know I won't come till later.
He comes with a sound as if he's taking a shit, unnnnhhh.

Afterwards, it's awkward. He leans forward, breathes hard, zips up.
"You?" he says.

"No," I say, shaking my head. He slides down the wall to sit beside
me on the rocks. One hand reaches out to rub my head briefly. After
that we don't touch, not intimately. We share a cigarette, enter email
addresses into phones. Later, in the hotel bathroom, I lie on the tiles
with a towel folded under my head and jack off.

None of this actually happens, mind you. Except for the last bit.

The guidebook says that Huê is considered the most beautiful city in Vietnam but I wouldn't know. Six days into our trip, I'm already tired of sightseeing. While my mother is photographing the citadel, I'm in an internet kiosk calling home. My lover and our friends in Australia are setting up for a queer New Year's Eve sex party, and I want to so badly to be there I can't sleep. But I do love the smell of Huê. The rain hasn't stopped since we arrived. It's like the clouds are sighing with relief after eating mouthfuls of grass. This is what I can smell at midnight on New Year's Eve in a backpacker bar, half full of tourists in fishermen's pants and half full of much better dressed locals.

I wasn't sure I wanted to come out at all but a drunk American firefighter from the hotel invited me along. I'm wary. After a beer and twenty minutes of his noxious (and sexist) monologue, I ditch him. I'm sitting on a barstool alone, trying to message home, and planning maybe to leave after I get a dance in when someone puts a pack of Vietnamese cigarettes down on the table in front of me. I look at the cigarettes and to the face of the boy lighting up. He's Vietnamese, wearing a gray t-shirt and jeans. The t-shirt is tight, showing off the strength of his shoulders, the neat compactness of his waist. His forehead is marked with horizontal lines. He smiles at me and I want a cigarette.

"Can I give you money for one of those?" I say. He's already pushing the pack towards me.

"No money," he says. "Take one."

His name is Hoa. He shakes my hand with a grave formality that undoes me, and then we're conversing as if we've been drinking together all night. Hoa speaks fluent English and I'm relieved, although this very act—assessment, relief—sucks me into colonialism. He introduces me to his friend, Thanh, shorter and skinnier in an even tighter t-shirt with a narrow red and green horizontal stripe. The three of us start dancing. But the music is so-so until the *boomp-bada, boomp-bada* of "Milkshake" thumps on. I've been longing for this all night, a muscular bass line up the spine flicking staccato into your hips, hands clicking to the bell sample on the four. The *la la, la la la. Warm it up. La la, la la la. The boys are waiting.* Hoa shakes his ass, his hips low, shoulders following the snap of the vocal. When he comes up, he catches my eye and holds it. He mimes grabbing a big handful of Afro, just like Kelis. His face radiates a confidence, a kind of fuck-you quality. Hard and intelligent but not mean. I watch him thinking *surely you're a fag* and as soon as I've thought it I know exactly why I wanted his cigarette. His eye catches mine again and I grin, holding his gaze. He doesn't look away. He smiles.

"How old are you?" he says when "Milkshake" ends. Unlike urban Melbourne, in Southeast Asia I seem to pass everywhere as male. My white skin camouflages me as yet another generic male tourist. I also pass as a young man, not a man in his thirties. When I tell people I'm thirty-two, I get raised eyebrows. Anyhow, I don't often travel like this, in hotels or on tours where such questions are part of the service. I've spent most of my traveling time in Bangkok doing research; none of my Bangkok friends are straight and they already know my secrets. Traveling with my mother is different. She's social, interested in hotel clerks, tour guides, other tourists, and they are interested back, intrigued by this nice, middle-aged, Australian woman and her son on holiday together. After age, other questions follow: "Where do you work? Do you have a girlfriend? Are you married?" Or to my mother: "Where is your husband?" The age and husband questions press us both against the innards of not being 'normal'. Conferring in a cramped Superior Twin at Brothers Hotel in Hanoi, my mother and I make a pact to tell anyone who asks that I'm 25 and that her husband is at home working.

Tonight I don't want to lie. I tell Hoa my real age. He frowns, and the creases in his forehead deepen. "You look much younger," he says. He doesn't ask if I'm married or if I have a girlfriend. I don't ask him if he does, either. Instead, I ask him about his work. He's a tour guide. It turns out we both majored in English Literature. He then went back to school to study tourist management. Aside from construction, tourism is the only industry with jobs here. "In Australia, anyone can get a job, right?" he says.

"No!" I laugh. "It's the same in Australia. You study English Literature, you still end up with a bad job, but a bad job with better pay."

Hoa sips his beer and looks at the floor. I see desire in his eyes for a place far away from here and it reminds me of the different desires white people bring here, and how much more money I have compared to him. "Australia. It's a good place," he says. He takes another cigarette from the pack and holds it out.

"No thanks," I say. "I already quit. Just sometimes I smoke."

"Good man," he nods. It comes out like it's straight from '40s noir, and Hoa says it without apparent irony but my ribs swell with pleasure. Oh, I want to be a good man. I want Hoa's forehead to corrugate again with the effort of assessing my character. I want us to exist in a black-and-white world where I'll play the bar piano and he'll stand by, deep in thought.

But this world is far from black-and-white. There are Christmas lights everywhere, the ceiling carpeted with flashing snowflakes. Above the pool table, a dancer knocks her head on the paper lantern light fitting. Some guy stands stationary in the throng to reach up and fix it. He can't, the fitting is broken, and when I look a minute later he's dancing again, holding the lantern up above the crowd with one hand. Outside it's raining and drops fly under the porch onto the windowsill. Hoa draws air dragons in front of my eyes. His hands skim close. "Magic," he says.

I make hand dragons back, countering his magic with my own. I feel calm, ecstatic. Weight evaporates off the surface of my skin. This is good. This is what New Year's Eve should be. Hoa lifts his arms and his t-shirt slides up. Underneath I can see his belly: dark reddish skin, sparse threads of black hair curling from the waistband of his jocks up towards his navel. I think about how his hipbones would feel under my palms. How his lips would taste. Then I look up to the drunk, straight, white boys and their 'Same Same' shirts and at all the hetero mating rituals taking place around us. It's not safe, not nearly.

But where is safe here? I don't even know. A guidebook talked of general disapproval of homosexuality, permissive karaoke bars in Hanoi, and "frank" cruising around Hoàn Kiam Lake. But these guides don't list the Vietnamese terms for queer, gay, lesbian... let alone trans. They don't say if it's even okay to ask. "Gay" doesn't describe what I want to say, especially about myself. Yet "gay" is what I go with in the end. Swallowing fear. Moving close.

"Can I ask you something personal?" We're close enough now so I don't have to yell. He shrugs, sure. I pause. "You're gay, right?"

At first it doesn't look good. His eyes close for a beat as if I'm about to punch him. I grin as wide as I can. "You don't have to tell me," I say. "But that's what I am."

His forehead does corrugate now. Maybe to find the right words. "I'm proud. Of myself. I don't hide anything." By now we're not dancing anymore. Hoa's head is bent so his ear can be close to my mouth. His chest is so near my face that if I leaned forward a couple of inches I could rest my head there.

"You're really cute," I say. "You want to go for a walk?"

His forehead smoothes out and he nods. We just go. Out on Lê Loi Street, the rain has cleared to a light mist. A knot of cyclo drivers wearing clear plastic rain ponchos are calling out to anyone who leaves. On the other side of the street is a park, and beyond that the gliding darkness of the Huong Giang, the Perfume River. When we're past the cyclo drivers, it's a little weird. There's less to say.

"Where can we go?" I say.

"The bridge," he says, stopping to point. He turns back to me, our hips butting up against each other, and then his tongue is inside my mouth and my hands are buried under his shirt in the muscular hollows under his shoulder blades. We walk under the bridge, we fuck, and then I run.

I don't ask him to go for a walk. Instead, with heterosexuals milling around us, I swallow fear again and blurt, "I want to tell you something about me." Not breathing. Reaching for the simplest way to say it. "I used to be a woman. But I changed, and now I'm male."

His head is still bent looking at the floor, ear close to mine. He's still. Then he looks me in the eyes. I see that he had no idea. The impact of this. Then, with the same careful attentiveness as before, he says, "I respect you." And then another pause, and, "I didn't know it was possible. I know men who become women," he clarifies, "but never the other way."

I can't explain to him right then why I'm telling him. That I don't want this to be a smug traveler's tale about how I went stealth and fooled some Vietnamese trick. That talking to him feels like home but that I don't want to invest in queerness to erase the differences between us. I don't know how to say that transmen can be faggots, too. These are words that work in my metropolis, not his. Or so I assume. Mostly right then I'm thinking that he's decided he doesn't want to fuck me. Maybe it's not true, but I tell myself I have to act as if it is.

Trying to refocus conversation on him, I say, "Do your parents know about you?" "We don't talk about it," he says. "I don't talk about it with anyone. Even my boss. She's a lesbian. We worked at the same company for two years before we found out about each other."

"Are there bars that you go to, that other gay people go to?" I ask. "No. There are no bars like that in Huê," he says, with a resigned smile. We talk more, maybe he asks me about surgery or hormones. Then he breaks off from talking. He looks at the table, where Thanh has propped himself on a barstool.

"You look tired," I say.

"Yes," he says, "I need to sit down." He sits, his back to me, takes out another cigarette. He rests his elbows on the table, rubs his eyes, puts his head in his hands. I keep dancing. The bar is less packed now. There's space to really move but I can't enjoy it. Hoa's back is bent as if he's carrying a weight. His shoulders are hunched. I want to walk up and embrace him from behind. I would wrap my fingers in the belt-loops at his hips, lean in to the curve of his back and put my mouth to the nape of his neck where his black hair was shortest. He would straighten like a thirsty plant given water and it would be okay.

But this is not going to happen. Thanh leans over and asks Hoa something in Vietnamese. They talk. At one point Thanh snorts with laughter. He looks over at me in a way that is still entirely friendly. But they have closed off, a little. Or maybe I have. The display on my phone reads 3:12 a.m. My mother and I are catching a train south in five hours. I walk up between Hoa and Thanh and say, "I should go. It's very late."

"What are you doing tomorrow?" says Thanh.

"I'm going to Da Nang on the train," I say. "I wish I could stay."

I turn to Hoa. He extends his hand to shake mine, and then we're hugging. "Thank you for dancing with me," I say, holding him.

He says, "It's good to meet you."

"And you," I say. "I'm glad I asked you for a cigarette." And then, I get it in fast, "You're really cute."

"Thank you," he says, and he's smiling. He kisses me goodbye on both cheeks.

Walking out of the bar I feel a mixture of arousal and sadness, but there's a freedom: *I told someone I'm trans, and he didn't freak out. I was myself.* At the hotel door, the shutters are down. I rap on the door and a teenager sleeping on a mattress in the lobby comes to open it.

"I'm sorry," I say. He shakes his head and wanders back to the mattress. I walk upstairs, sit in the stairwell, and dial my friend Joni in Australia. This time I get through. It's 6 a.m. there. Her drugs have worn off and she's sitting on the pavement outside the club. It's good to talk to her. Later, I walk into the hotel room. My mother is snoring. In the bathroom, door locked, I lie on the floor and fold a towel under my head.

Get A Job!
Max Wolf Valerio

When I told my dad I was becoming a man, he declared, "Now you're going to have to make your money like a man!"

I am proud to say I did not sneer back, "Dad, that's so *binary* of you!" I sensed that I was receiving a secret handshake of manhood. Even if it made me cringe, my dad was telling me something important about the male role to speed me on my way to success.

As a perennial outsider, even as female, I modeled myself after my counterculture heroes who rebelled against the male role of work. Men who rarely worked steady, or who worked adventurous, exotic jobs that carried them to foreign lands or immersed them in gritty streetwise experiences. Jobs they would later write about, or sing about with the rhythms of that working time as a backdrop. Guys who worked with a cast of strange characters and lived nearly dissolute, wandering crazed lives lit up by the need to create, to go beyond the surface of the ordinary: Jack Kerouac and Allen Ginsberg in the Merchant Marine; Henry Miller who gave up his family and a management position at a telegraph company, fleeing New York to sleep on couches and write novels in Paris. Men who lived strange, mystic inner lives at the edges of poverty, punctuated with manic creative antics and adventures... poets.

I was in dangerous waters. One girlfriend I dated alerted me early on. She said that she would think twice about dating a man who did not have money. She would not be the last. In fact, this early-in-my-transition girlfriend provided the opening gambit. Her remark, delivered as a nearly offhand observation of personal requirements and attitudes, would prove prophetic. I've since learned that women care a lot more about what's in my wallet than what's in my pants.

Another woman I dated soon after softly stunned me when she told me of some troubling thoughts that had surfaced. As she lay next to me, unable to sleep one night, she reflected on her love for me, and like a devil twin to her passion, her doubts arose: "What if this guy's a total bum?" Luckily for me her answer to this pressing doubt was an affirmation of her most positive feelings, "It doesn't matter I love him anyway."

I was grateful for that, ah, vote of confidence? But still troubled that she had even worried that I was..." a bum. " A bum?

But, you know, I kinda was. And bums were my heroes, after all. Poet bums, painter bums, mystic bums, sex bomb gigolo bums. But was being a bum the best way for me to navigate my future?

My most recent girlfriend would bring the riddle full circle and lay bare its requisite parts. I have had many jobs in my life, and most have not paid well. As I stated earlier, my goals have been artistic and not financial. And so, when I was 46, there I was working a part-time contract job on the phone from home, generating leads for software companies. I made around $12 an hour, and worked sporadically with no benefits. Not exactly Lee Iacocca. My girl at the time, Anna, had been with me for nine months and things were becoming more serious. Well, they must have been because one night she declared, "I don't want to be with a man who's always broke!"

We were just sitting there, leaning into each other, comfy, getting ready for bed. I didn't know what to say. I had never borrowed money; we went out a lot in spite of my being generally strapped for cash. She became adamant, almost screaming, "I don't want to be with a man who is always broke!"

Anna explained later that when she was strictly dating women, money didn't matter as much to her in a partner. A femme, she would even slip money to butches under the table to give the impression to the waitperson that the butch was paying, even if the butch could not pay for them both. The appearance of gallant masculinity toward a feminine voluptuary, pampered and possessed, was important... but in that case, with a butch, an illusion was sufficient. However, I was a man and that meant I had to... man up. "Men," Anna declared, "are providers and protectors." She wanted security and she wanted it now.

This demand struck me as totally unfair. And, of course, in some sense it was and remains so. But life is not fair. And if I was honest, I had to admit that in middle age, I had gotten sick of being poor. Poverty no longer felt as poetic.

So I tried. I posted my resume on Craigslist and within forty-eight hours I had eleven responses from a myriad of software and tech companies including… Apple Computer. Most were offering me salaries upwards of 65K with bountiful commissions up to 30K on top of that, and there could be more – they claimed the sky was the limit. I was stunned. And, yes, I got one of those high-paying sales development jobs.

Anna was relieved and happy. Later, she realized that she had been PMSing when she had made her demands. Even so, Anna was glad she had, and now realized the purpose for which her feminine mood swings were created… to whip her boyfriend's butt into tiptop shape. I realized that men often settle for less in their lives, but with a woman to impress they will work harder and try harder, and maybe, that's actually not such a bad thing. Traditionally, men have had to prove themselves worthy of a woman. Sometimes great things happen for them and for the world when they try.

As I settled into my newfound prosperity, Anna declared that she wanted to manage my money for me now. Male friends that I trusted told me that all of the most successful men they knew let their wives manage their money. I pondered this… Anna said, "Think about it. No hurry."

First, she wanted me to buy her a corset.

About the Authors

Aren Z. Aizura is a writer and professor based in Philadelphia. He was awarded his PhD in Cultural Studies from the University of Melbourne in 2009. His work has been published in *Self-Organizing Men: Conscious Masculinities in Time and Space* and a variety of scholarly journals.

Ashley Altadonna is a bi-curious transexual filmmaker living in Milwaukee, Wisconsin. Her films, *Whatever Suits You* and *Playing With Gender*, have screened at film festivals from San Francisco to London. She is also the owner of Tall Lady Pictures. She lives with her amazing wife, Maria, and their two cats, Gatsby and Darcy.

Patch Avery can be found rehearsing poetry while vacuuming. He's a stay-at-home dad with a propensity to write at 3 a.m. He is currently working on his first novel between bedtimes stories and trips to the park. He resides in Seattle with his partner of nine years and three young sons.

Caitlyn Benoit lives near Saint Louis with her partner, Allison, and their dog, Tasha. Katie has been writing and performing music since age 13, and has produced and remixed music since 1999. Katie is also a staunch advocate for the rights of all people, regardless of background.

Cooper Lee Bombardier is a visual artist, writer, and performer living in Portland, Oregon where he is finishing his masters degree in writing and publishing. Cooper loves working with his hands, lifting weights, growing sideburns,hiking with his buddies and his dogs; and he believes in the power of karaoke to unite communities.

James Diamond has been diagnosed with bipolar disorder. He's always been involved with media-making and activism. After struggling with the intense highs and lows of bipolar disorder, he is now taking Western meds, becoming an actor, and is way saner than he ever knew was possible.

Morty Diamond is a trans artist working in a variety of media, from performance art to the written word. He is the editor of the anthology *From the Inside Out: Radical Gender Transformation, FTM and Beyond*. He has directed and produced two films, *Trannyfags* and *Trans Entities*. Morty is currently studying Sociology and Gender Studies at UC Berkeley.

Imani Henry is an Activist, Writer, and Artist. His writing has appeared in several publications including *Does Your Mama Know*, and *Voices Rising: Celebrating 20 years of Black LGBT Writing*. Imani is also a journalist for the progressive weekly newspaper, *Workers' World*. He is proud to be Caribbean transexual male living in the Republic of Brooklyn, NY.

Jakob Hero is a clergy candidate with the Metropolitan Community Churches, and a seminary student at Pacific School of Religion. He and his partner, Patrick Califia, live in Berkeley, California.

Silas Howard (writer, director, musician) co-directed his first feature, *By Hook Or By Crook*, with Harry Dodge. The indie classic was a 2002 Sundance Film Festival premiere and five-time Best Feature winner. Howard received an MFA in directing at UCLA. For eight years, Howard toured with the band, Tribe 8. Howard's writing is also featured in *Without a Net* and *Live Through This: On Creativity and Self-Destruction*.

Bryn Kelly is a beauty school drop-out and multimedia artist of Appalachian extraction. She organizes grassroots support for Brooklyn-based movements toward economic justice, reproductive health, and HIV education. Two years after writing this piece, Bryn broke up with that guy, got her Saturn return, and became a big lesbian. Seriously.

Jennie Kermode is content director at Eye For Film and author of The Orpheus Industry. She is also a campaigner on LGBT and disability rights issues. She lives in Glasgow, Scotland.

Kai Kohlsdorf is a drag king/queen cum entertainer currently researching trans discourse (historical and current) and what sex, popular culture, and porn have to do with it for a master's thesis. He is a trans/genderqueer educator teaching undergraduate classes, speaking at conferences and other venues, and co-running a tranny group around town. His gender is a daily discussion; right now he's genderqueer/trans.

Sassafras Lowrey is a genderqueer high femme author, artist, and activist. Sassafras edited the award-winning *Kicked Out* anthology, and the author of *GSA to Marriage: Stories of a Life Lived Queerly*. Sassafras lives in NYC with hir partner, two cats, and a princess dog.

Amos Mac is a writer and photographer who bounces between the neighborhoods of Bushwick and the Mission chasing photographic affairs and inspiration. His photos have appeared on the pages of *Cutter Photozine*. He is the co-editor of *Original Plumbing* magazine.

Glenn Marla is a New York City performance artist. Marla's work has been featured at the Culture Project, Theater for the New City, HERE Arts Center, P.S. 122, Joe's Pub, Ars Nova, Dixon Place, Galapagos Art Space, Bowery Poetry Club, 3rd Ward, and Abrons Arts Center. .

Dee Ouellette is a mom and a woman and a tranny. She is a light-skinned mix of French, Slovak, and indigenous to Turtle Island. She prefers Annie Sprinkle to Ann Coulter, and Castro to Bush. She recently published *the chrysalis in the kitchen* to raise funds for her second surgery.

Megan K. Pickett is an associate professor of physics at Lawrence University in Appleton, Wisconsin. Before coming to Lawrence, she was a research associate at NASA's Ames Research Center and a professor at Valparaiso University and Purdue University Calumet. Pickett lives in Appleton with her partner, Lynne, and a large, lazy cat.

Phyllis Pseudonym (not her real name) is terribly pleased with the photo on her new green card. An MTF artist living and working in New York City, Phyllis remains happily married and deeply in love, though not always with the same person. "City Hall" is her first published fiction.

Timea Quon was born November 8, 1983 in Vancouver, British Columbia where she still reside s (and probably will till the day she dies).

MTF transexual. Began transitioning offically in 2003 and started RLE and hormones in 2005. Aspiring writer, erotic entertainer, musician, and professional boxer.

Joelle Ruby Ryan has completed hir doctorate in American Culture Studies at Bowling Green State University. Hir research interests include trans identity, feminism, sex work, fat studies, and media culture. S/he is the author of *Gender Quake: Poems* and the producer of the video, *TransAmazon*.

Sam Silverman is a screenwriter and specialist in casual fine dining. He recently moved to Los Angeles to pursue his dreams of making million-dollar movies on a shoestring budget. He has one too many master's degrees and Plan B has recently become "wine expert."

Vera Sepulveda is a California native who enjoys a simple life, working as a receptionist and library assistant in San Francisco. Comfortable in the gray areas between male and female, Vera has lived in roles ranging from cowboy to bridesmaid. Her essay, "Confessions of a She-Male Merchant Marine" can be found in *Finding the Real Me* (Jossey-Bass).

Julia Serano is an Oakland, California-based writer, spoken word artist, and trans activist. She is the author of *Whipping Girl: A Transexual Woman on Sexism and the Scapegoating of Femininity.* Julia's writing has appeared in anthologies including *BITCHfest* and *Word Warriors*, and in magazines such as *Out, make/shift,* and *Transgender Tapestry.*

Max Wolf Valerio is an iconoclastic poet and writer. His memoir, *The Testosterone Files,* primarily covers his first five years on testosterone. He has appeared in many documentaries including *You Don't Know Dick, Gendernauts* and *Max* (from the feature *Female Misbehavior*), and *Octopus Alarm.*

Shawna Virago is celebrated as a trans pioneer in music, filmmaking, and activism. Ms. Virago is also director of TrannyFest, a film festival dedicated to supporting work made by and for transgender and genderqueer people. She is a founding member of TransAction, the police accountability group.

Cameron Thomas Whitley is a transgender guy from a small town in Colorado. He currently resides in Brooklyn with his finance, Melanie, and their Yorkshire terrier, Pal. Although he came of age in the West, his days are currently spent working as a financial officer and freelance writer in New York City.

L. Winterset is a tranny who lives with his wife in the upper Midwest. He seeks to live his life manifesting the belief that there are an infinite number of ways to express gender identities. "Unicorn" is the first piece he has written about his experiences with gender.

Taylor Xavier is a queer transman, a sex educator, and a third generation writer. A dirty rambler originally from Texas, he has called many places home and currently lives in Oakland with his dog, Jackson. He can often be found slinging sex toys, studying graphic design, or making coffee and migas.